by
**Walter A. Henrichsen**
and
**William N. Garrison**

# LAYMAN, LOOK UP!

## GOD HAS A PLACE
## FOR YOU

**ZONDERVAN
PUBLISHING HOUSE**

OF THE ZONDERVAN CORPORATION
GRAND RAPIDS, MICHIGAN 49506

*Layman, Look Up!*
Copyright © 1983 by The Zondervan Corporation
Grand Rapids, Michigan

**Library of Congress Cataloging in Publication Data**

Henrichsen, Walter A.
    Layman, look up!

    1. Laity.  I.  Garrison, William N.  II.  Title.
BV4525.H49   1983      262'.15      82-21838
ISBN 0-310-37721-8

Unless otherwise indicated, Scripture references are quoted from *The Holy Bible, The New International Version,* copyright 1978 by the New York International Bible Society.

Designed by Kim Koning
Edited by Edward Viening

*Printed in the United States of America*

83  84  85  86  87  88 — 10  9  8  7  6  5  4  3  2  1

# CONTENTS

## DEFINITION

*"Laity* . . . the people outside a particular profession, as distinguished from those belonging to it."

Particularly, in religious terms, "not a member of the clergy."

# PROLOGUE

A layman from Oklahoma City recently declared, "We are in the midst of a second reformation. The first had to do with getting the *Scriptures* into the hands of the laity. This one has to do with getting the *ministry* into the hands of the laity."

It will be left to historians to decide whether the last half of the twentieth century was a time of spiritual awakening in the United States, but it is apparent that God is at work during these troubled times. The laity are the vanguard of the action. It is our hope, and the purpose of this book, that the ministry of the ordinary layman representing Christ in the marketplace will be encouraged.

There are certain impediments, which if removed, will give impetus to this movement. Calling attention to them may contribute to their removal, freeing people to use their vocations as their pulpits, and we will explore these impediments in the course of the book.

Briefly stated, the problem is that there are a cacophony of Christian voices calling the average layman to this or that enterprise. Each competes for his time, gifts, and money. Each seeks to herd him into an organizational corral and place a brand on him. Poised above the noise and din is the institutional church insisting that all legitimate ministry should be the outgrowth of its programs and that all fruit should accrue to its benefit. This competition for the allegiance of the Christian laity hinders their ability to use their business and community as the platform for their ministry. This fierce competition is the product of an inadequate view of the *ministry, church* and *organizations.*

## Ministry

Foundational to an understanding of the ministry is the New Testament teaching concerning the priesthood of the believer. Every believer has both the right and responsibility to be an ambassador of Christ.

In raising up the functioning layman to be His ambassador, God uses a variety of influences in his life. Family, youth leaders, pastors, teachers—all have a contribution in helping him become a productive disciple. Thus, he is never the product of any single individual or institution. It is the Holy Spirit that orchestrates the process and brings it to fruition.

Nor can the contribution made in this functioning disciple's life be measured or controlled. Equal time and effort does not necessarily produce equal results. Most, if not all the growth, is qualitative rather than quantitative. Qualitative change can be observed but not measured.

When the organization or local church claims ownership of this layman, competition results. It loses sight of the fact that he is the product of God, not man, and it succumbs to the worldly temptation of evaluating its own worth by taking credit for his becoming a productive man in the Body of Christ.[1]

## Church

Jesus said, "I will build my church." There is no scriptural mandate for the believer to build the church. The mandate is to witness and preach the gospel. People do not build churches; they institutionalize the church Jesus builds.

Prior to the Reformation all that was taking place for Christ in a geographical locale was called the church. Although it was institutionalized, it was under one organization with competition for the most part eliminated. The Protestant Reformation fed the competitive instinct with its plethora of organizations.

The church is not any single institution or organization. It is an organism brought into existence by Jesus Christ. There are *examples* of the institutional church in the New Testament, but there is no *command* to institutionalize the church. The church as an organization is descriptive, not prescriptive, in the Bible.

Because the church is an organism brought into

---

[1]There are instances in the Scriptures, such as the Book of Acts, where the author calls attention to numerical gains, e.g. "and there were added to them about three thousand souls." This is the observable impact of what the Holy Spirit did through the *whole* church. Today, however, when you read someone's newsletter or magazine and statistics are quoted, the impression is that this is what the Holy Spirit did through that person or organization. Such thinking loses focus of the fact that people are led to Christ and discipled through the whole Body and not through any single individual organization.

existence by God, all that God is doing in a city is the church. No single organization can lay claim to the title "The Church," and no Christian group or organization can be excluded from being called part of the church.

An inadequate understanding of this is confusing to the laity. He sees the church competing over his loyalty and finances and is unsure of how to relate.

## Organizations

Organizations are not evil or counterproductive to the cause of Christ. They are legitimate means to an end but should never be an end in themselves. Organizations can become very useful as vehicles for the ministry.

In creating them, however, it should be understood that God is in the business of redeeming people, not institutions. Organizations are not eternal, people are! Thus, expending emotional energy on their preservation should be avoided. Use them, take care of them, but don't give your life for them.

When a biblical view of institutions is embraced, it frees one to co-labor with God in that which is dear to His heart, namely people. The ministry of the laity is the ministry of people investing in the lives of people. To the degree that organizations foster this ministry they should be encouraged.[2]

---

[2]When they understand that those involved with them are the product of a variety of institutions and people, they cease competing and appreciate all ministries that are contributing to the cause of Christ.

When they begin to compete for the loyalty of people, they become counterproductive.

In these days of unprecedented opportunity, the laity's functioning ~~hws~~ God's ~~priests~~ should be affirmed and encouraged. God has called the various ministries into being to do this task.

# CHAPTER 1

# WHAT IS EXPECTED OF THE LAITY?

*The traditional role assigned to the laity does not comply with what God expects of the laity.*

Switzerland, 1974.

Evangelical leaders from around the world were gathered for the Lausanne International Congress on World Evangelization. It was "laymen" night as business and professional men formed a panel to discuss the role of laymen in the task of world evangelism.

The U.S. representative, a real estate investor with a commitment to serving God, presented an ultimatum to the evangelical world that laymen such as he would no longer be content with the traditional role assigned to them by religious leaders.

He indicated that a "good" layman has traditionally been asked to do four things:

"1. Regularly attend all church functions,

2. Liberally give money in support of the church's program,

3. Support all church programs established by the leadership,

4. And adhere to the '11th commandment,' which is 'Don't rock the boat'."

The audience responded with easy and quick laughter. They had understood, for the role that the U.S. representative rejected by caricature is all too obviously the accepted role of a good layman.

Does the local assembly truly desire a compliant role for the laity? Does the clergy believe that the highest development the individual can achieve is to conform to the institutional aims of the local organization? If so, that American realtor, as a "representative" layman, is out of step, for he feels there can be a different and more exciting function for the laity. So do tens of thousands of other men and women. So do we.

The laity, by the very nature of their positions in life, move in the mainstream of a society that is broken and needy. The ministry of reconciliation has been given to the layman. *Increasingly, men and women across the country and around the world are determined to have a significant role in God's program for the church.*

Many local assembly leaders, however, have

given an inadequate sense of mission to its members. If a biblically literate person participates only in the four-point program outlined above, it leaves him unsatisfied, because the scriptural mandate that says the believer should function in the marketplace as God's ambassador is irreconcilable with the role that has been all to often given to the laity.

Several years ago a group of business men in a major city began meeting in weekly Bible study. One interested man seemed reluctant to commit himself as the group was forming. In private conversation he finally confessed that he was the senior layman in his local congregational government and was embarrassed lest people discover his abysmal ignorance of the Bible. No more requirement was made of him in becoming a congregational officer than was asked of him in his service club! Tragically, he is not atypical!

The laity want a challenge!

They want to be fully equipped to do the ministry!

In this book we want to show how today's Christian layman can move from the uninspiring role that has been assigned to him and into having a rich, in-depth, effective ministry for God.

## God Has a Place for the Layman Today

The international "movement" of jogging is analogous with what we would like to see happen in the kingdom of God.

In many nations people are jogging for exercise. There are millions of runners in this country alone, very few of whom jogged before Dr. Kenneth H. Cooper wrote *Aerobics* in 1968. He started a movement of effective physical fitness.

The majority of the joggers we see along the highways, on the sidewalks, and in the parks are *doing it on their own.* They are not members of "jogging" clubs. This is one of the values of Dr. Cooper's aerobics program. You don't have to join anything to do it! You can have good fitness simply by jogging through your neighborhood streets.

We would like to see a similar movement, spiritually!

Lay followers of Christ who are disciples in the battlefield are eager, by the hundreds of thousands, to serve God in their sphere of influence. They want to be part of His program for history. But, for a number of reasons, they are being denied the larger part of the action they could be having in the marketplace today. This shouldn't be. God's plan includes them . . . in fact, it is centrally focused on *lay men and women.*

The purpose of this small book is to challenge and show discipled lay people how they can join a groundswell movement for Christ simply by ministering right where they live and work. Just as a jogger doesn't need to be a professional runner to get physically fit, neither does the dedicated disciple have to be a "professional religious worker." In fact, that could, in some cases, be detrimental.

The need today is not for new, improved structures. God *is* at work. The need is to identify what He is doing and join Him. Jesus said, "Whoever serves me must follow me; and where I am, my servant also will be" (John 12:26). The servant of Jesus is working where He is working. One man put it this way: "Find out what the Holy Spirit has burning and pour fuel on the flame!"

All one needs do is channel his fervor for Christ in the proper direction, and he can join with others who today are making an impact on this society for God. This book is designed for the thinking, Christ-centered lay person who seeks to serve God in the day-to-day "real" world—RIGHT WHERE HE OR SHE IS!

## FOR DISCUSSION

1. List three or four things you feel your congregation regularly expects of you. Are these compatible with your personal ministry desires?

2. Do you agree that the four things the "good" local assembly laymen are required to do as expressed by the U.S. representative in Lausanne are an accurate appraisal? What would you add? What would you delete?

3. Have you personally been expected to do any or all of these four things?

4. If you are an officer in your congregation, do you feel scripturally qualified?

5. What would you like to do in your sphere of influence that you feel you are unable to do because of lack of support by your congregation?

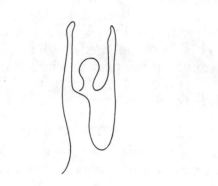

# PART 1

# LAYMEN AND THE MINISTRY

The person who gets involved in God's work must embrace God's value system. The world measures success by what we get . . . God measures it by what we give. The world's measure is by the people we manipulate . . . God's, by the people we serve. Take the world's system and invert it.

**CHAPTER 2**

# Sheep
# and Disciples

*As a follower of Christ, you are a
"sheep" or a "disciple." All followers are His sheep, but not all sheep
are His disciples.*

One cool, spring morning seven of Jesus' disciples sat with Him on the shore of the Sea of
Galilee. They were having breakfast of fried fish
and bread. Jesus had died, been buried, and had
risen from the dead. This was the third time He
had visited His disciples in His resurrected body.

After eating, Jesus and Peter had an unusual
conversation that has a vital bearing on our lives
today. Three times Jesus asked Peter if he loved

Him. Each time Peter said yes. After each answer, Jesus told him to feed His sheep (or lambs).

This question and command made such a deep impression on Peter that he admonished the elders in his first letter to them, "Feed the flock of God which is among you . . ." (1 Peter 5:2 KJV).

## Who Are the Sheep?

In the conversation with Peter, Jesus referred to "My sheep." Who are these people?

Jesus explains who His "sheep" are in the parable of the Good Shepherd in John 10. He says the sheep *know* the voice of the Shepherd and follow only Him. The Shepherd also *knows* each of His sheep by name.

John 10:9–11 says, "I am the gate; whoever enters through me will be saved. He will come in and go out, and find pasture. The thief comes only to steal and kill and destroy; I have come that they may have life, and have it to the full. I am the good shepherd. The good shepherd lays down his life for the sheep."

Jesus is the Shepherd. All who are saved (born again) are the sheep. The only requirement for being a sheep is salvation. Over and over again the Scriptures say that salvation is a free gift based on the grace of God. It is not obtained by the believer's performance, but by Jesus' performance on the believer's behalf.

## Who, Then, Are Disciples?

A disciple of Christ is a sheep—and more. He is a follower who, naturally, is saved, but who has

24

also gone on to fulfill other requirements demanded by Jesus of those who wish to become His disciples:

*A disciple continues in the Word:* "'If you hold to my teaching, you are really my disciples'" (John 8:31).

*A disciple loves:* "'All men will know that you are my disciples if you love one another'" (John 13:35).

*A disciple bears fruit:* "'This is to my Father's glory, that you bear much fruit, showing yourselves to be my disciples'" (John 15:8).

These are just some of the key characteristics of a disciple. Perhaps the classic passage on the requirements of being a disciple is Luke 14:25–33:

> Large crowds were traveling with Jesus, and turning to them he said: "If anyone comes to me and does not hate his father and mother, his wife and children, his brothers and sisters—yes, even his own life—he cannot be my disciple. And anyone who does not carry his cross and follow me cannot be my disciple.
>
> "Suppose one of you wants to build a tower. Will he not first sit down and estimate the cost to see if he has enough money to complete it? For if he lays the foundation and is not able to finish it, everyone who sees it will ridicule him, saying, 'This fellow began to build and was not able to finish.'
>
> "Or suppose a king is about to go to war against another king. Will he not first sit down and consider whether he is able with ten thousand men to oppose the one coming against him with twenty thousand? If he is not able, he will send a delega-

tion while the other is still a long way off and will ask for terms of peace. In the same way, any of you who does not give up everything he has cannot be my disciple."

Discipleship is obligatory, but is not a condition for salvation. Being born again is based on Jesus' performance; being a disciple is based on the believer's performance. Though all sheep are called to discipleship, not all respond.

There are many reasons why people don't respond to the challenge to become disciples: immaturity, problem centeredness, lack of understanding, worldliness—just to name a few.

Failure to distinguish between being sheep and disciples is to blur the concept of law and grace. Salvation is a gift from God. A proper response to that gift is discipleship, but failure to become a disciple does not negate salvation.

What then is the disciple's responsibility toward those believers (sheep) who never become disciples? He is to feed them! They are God's sheep, washed in His blood and bound for heaven. Their primary feeding often comes from the pastor, for this is one of his functions. It is what Jesus told Peter to do. It is what Peter told the church elders to do. "Feed the sheep!"

## The Functioning Disciple

Most sheep receive their basic feeding from the Word from the pastor on Sunday, but the average disciple gets most of his spiritual food from three other principle sources—these are, in fact, the same sources where the pastor gets *his* feeding.

*First* and foremost, the disciple is fed from his own time in the Word. Jesus said, "If ye continue in my word then are ye my disciples" (John 8:32 KJV). Paul followed this with the admonition, "Let the word of Christ dwell in you richly . . ." (Col. 3:16 KJV). The disciple is one who knows how to feed himself from the Word of God and is doing it on a regular basis.

*Second,* the disciple is fed by his peers—that band of men and women with whom he shares a common vision. This occurs in small group Bible studies, in conversation over lunch, or other personal time together: these are times of intense interaction and learning.

Recently, we were with a group of businessmen at a restuarant having a cup of coffee. We had just finished an evangelistic luncheon at which one of the men had spoken. As we talked, we shared what God had been teaching each of us from the Word.

The men were excited about discussing evangelism and discipleship. They were encouraging each other as they shared their experiences and told of the fresh directions they were receiving from the Word. They were men of varied denominational affiliations and their individual involvements in their local church situations differed greatly. Some were minimally involved; others highly involved. They were growing disciples.

To hear these men describe how they applied the Scriptures to daily situations in the marketplace made it a particularly rich time of spiritual feeding that day.

*Third,* the disciple feeds from the books and magazines he reads, the conferences and seminars he attends, and the tapes to which he listens. This mode of learning is more passive than the first two, but it does constitute valuable times of growth. Church and Sunday school attendance is included in this third category.

What does this say about the pastor's role in the life of the disciple? Is there a role? Yes, and a most strategic one. Here is how Paul explains this relationship:

> It was he who gave some to be apostles, some to be prophets, some to be evangelists, and some to be pastors and teachers, to prepare God's people for works of service, so that the body of Christ may be built up until we all reach unity in the faith and in the knowledge of the Son of God and become mature, attaining to the whole measure of the fullness of Christ (Eph. 4:11–13).

These gifted men (including the pastors or shepherds) equip the disciples ("prepare God's people for works of service"), so that they may do the work of the ministry. Although the Sunday sermon does help in the discipling process, a thirty minute lecture is not the same as equipping men for the ministry.

Just as all sheep are called to be disciples and not all respond, so all pastors are called to "make disciples," but not all do it. The laity (disciples in the marketplace) need "on-the-job training" to enable them to effectively do the work of the ministry. This passage in Ephesians suggests that they get this training from a *variety* of gifted people, only one of whom is the pastor.

## The Disgruntled Layman/Disciple

Many laymen view their relationship with their local congregation as unsatisfactory. A frequent complaint they have is "My pastor is not feeding me." This is a doubtful complaint, often reflecting a misunderstanding of the main role of the pastor. The pastor is not to direct his Sunday feeding primarily to the disciple . . . but to the sheep, in fulfillment of Jesus' command in John 21. This is a process the disciple should be participating in, not criticizing.

Disciples especially must be careful not to develop unrealistic expectations of their pastors. Much of the suspicion and discontent existing between local pastors and parachurch ministers arises because of a minunderstanding about the role each of them is to fulfill while exercising his particular gifts.

The disciple shouldn't expect the pastor to feed him. He should ask himself, rather, if the pastor is feeding the sheep (those who have not yet demonstrated a desire or spiritual maturity to pursue discipleship). If the pastor were to satisfy only the needs of the disciples in the congregation, he would be failing in his responsibility to feed the sheep. The pastor's sermons for disciples would invariably presuppose much understanding and knowledge that the sheep in the congregation do not have. But if this were to happen, the listening disciple, who may already have heard these teachings in his own developing process, would instinctively compare the pastor's presentation with the best one he heard in the past. The Bible-teaching local church can fall into this pitfall.

To the layman /disciple involved in a personal ministry in the marketplace, caution must be given to never adversely comment on the quality of the pastor's preaching. This could be magnified among the sheep and have serious repercussions.

Would-be disciples who act like sheep and make demands for themselves, which sheep could be expected to make, are often the root cause of the type of problems revealed in the New Testament Corinthian church.

Why then should the disciple even go to the Sunday services? Hebrews 10:25 says, "Let us not give up meeting together, as some are in the habit of doing, but let us encourage one another—and all the more as you see the Day approaching." He is told to do it.

The answer is further found in Acts 2:46–47:

Every day they continued to meet together in the temple courts. They broke break in their homes and ate together with glad and sincere hearts, praising God and enjoying the favor of all the people. And the Lord added to their number daily those who were being saved.

This explains that they worshiped, broke bread, and fellowshiped with one another. These are the main ingredients of the Sunday service and the reason why the disciple gathers with his brothers and sisters in Christ. He assembles with believers to worship, to share the Lord's table, for fellowship, and to support his pastor in the ministry of feeding the sheep.

A major point of this book will be to explain how the disciple in the marketplace can and does get equipped for his personal ministry, since he cannot rely primarily on the regular Sunday meetings.

## Complementing Ministries

The ministries of the laity and pastor cannot be reconciled apart from an appreciation of each. God has called them to *different ministries*. The need is for mutual understanding and the elimination of competition.

This could be polarized by saying that laymen make disciples and pastors feed the sheep. But this is not entirely true, for laymen also feed the sheep and pastors do make disciples. But each has his distinctive role in his particular ministry. Harmony results when these distinctives are understood and appreciated. The various ministries need to be supportive of one another.

### FOR DISCUSSION

1. Are you a sheep or a disciple? Explain why.
2. If you are a sheep, what measurable steps can you take to become a disciple?
3. Are you expecting too much of your local congregation? If so, how can you change your high expectations?
4. What are some practical ways you can foster a movement of the laity where you are?

# CHAPTER 3

# A STUDY OF TWO TYPES OF LAYMEN

*A so-called "worldly" Christian has a ministry that is impacting his sphere of influence, while another, who conforms to the image of a "good Christian layman," has an anemic ministry among his peers. How does this develop? What can be done to help both men?*

## The Story of Bill, Who Has a "Worldly" Lifestyle

Bill is an executive in a tobacco firm in a large metropolitan area. He and his wife, Carol, came to Christ five years ago in a Billy Graham Crusade.

Bill's commitment to Christ was total. The entire family experienced change, and they began attending a strong evangelical congregation.

We met Bill through a mutual friend and began developing a relationship. One day when we met his pastor, the pastor expressed deep concern for Bill and his family. He felt they had not grown appreciably since joining his assembly. He said Bill had not changed jobs, he still smoked, and that he and his wife kept liquor in their home. Furthermore, they were still part of the "world," in that they socialized with their non-Christian friends. In general, the pastor felt that they lived a "worldly lifestyle."

We were interested in this situation and prayed for an opportunity to talk to Bill. That evening we were invited to his home for dinner.

Bill told us about his day's activities. The single most important event to him was a conversation about Jesus Christ he had had with a fellow executive in the tobacco firm. On several occasions Bill had witnessed to him, but today was different. The man's marriage was about to dissolve and, in desperation, he sought Bill for help. Over lunch at the downtown businessmen's club, Bill led the man to Christ.

We then met Bill's wife, Carol, and their three children. The children were warm, positive, and absolutely charming. The love and concern they expressed toward one another made us pray that our children would develop as well as these had.

After dinner, some friends came over to visit Bill and Carol. In the course of the conversation, they related how Bill had led them to Christ a year earlier. The next day Bill invited us to a downtown club for lunch and asked if we would give our story of how we met Christ to a dozen or so of his friends. Bill didn't emcee the luncheon. A man named Bob did. We sat next to Bob, and while eating lunch he told us how Bill had introduced him to Christ two years earlier!

### The Story of Doug, Who Has a "Christian" Lifestyle

Doug and Jane live in the same city as Bill and Carol. Born and raised in a godly home, Doug went to a "Christian" college, married a born-again girl, and moved to this city where he serves as president of the utility company.

He attends a small, but good congregation in his community where he serves as the leading elder on the Board. He teaches Sunday school, is the confidant of the pastor, and is heavily involved in other congregational activities. There is no doubt about Doug being committed to Christ. In fact, he and Jane often talk of leaving the business world to go overseas as missionaries. If anything, Doug feels guilty because he isn't doing more for God.

Because of his desire to excel for God, Doug invited us to spend a few days with him—to observe what he was doing and to make suggestions on how he could penetrate his community for Christ.

It became immediately apparent that he had a vast network of business contacts throughout the metropolitan area. He knew the mayor very well, was on a first-name basis with the governor of his state, worked closely with all the key business executives and was highly respected by all.

That evening we met the group of men with whom Doug meets weekly in his home. They were all from the same local congregation—but there were no men from Doug's business or even from his neighborhood. During the sharing time, each man told what he was doing and how they were attempting the penetration of their city with the gospel. Their primary outreach was passing out tracts, as well as doing some calling for the pastor.

It was obvious that Doug had compartmentalized his life between the secular and spiritual and wasn't sure if he wanted to take the risk necessary to mix the two.

### Contrast or Harmony?

In many respects Bill and Doug are complete opposites. The former has come out of the world; the latter out of the local assembly. Through the years Bill has developed a rapport and ease with his non-Christian friends. *It is precisely at this point of his being a friend of publicans and sinners that the local congregation has problems with him.* His pastor would never say it is "wrong" to be friends with the uncommitted. It is the "price" the pastor feels Bill has to pay to do it that is objectionable. The fact that Bill isn't transgressing any of the scriptural commands is overlooked. So, also, is the fact that Bill's individual penetration of the world system for Christ is deeper and more fruitful than the rest of the local assembly's combined!

In contrast, Doug is a model member of the congregation. He is well-grounded in the Word and has a lifestyle that makes him a comfortable part of the established assembly. It isn't as though he has no contact with men at work, for scores of uncommitted businessmen know and admire Doug. It is just that they don't know his secret of successful living. He doesn't swear and always bows his head before meals to say grace. His business ethics are impeccable. But he is unable to relate his faith to his business associates. The ease with which Bill, the "worldly" Christian, relates his faith in Christ to the totality of life is a wonder to Doug and fills him with guilt.

The pressure the world exerts on people to conform is fierce, but so is the pressure of the local congregation that their members must conform to its image of how lay people must act. As long as Bill and Carol attend the "pure" assembly, there will be a steady undercurrent of pressure to conform to a more "acceptable" lifestyle.

For the average person in Bill's position it takes about two years to eliminate all the "questionable" habits, sever the non-Christian friendships, and retreat into the Christian ghetto. Then, very soon, the rehabilitated "Bills" begin to carry the same guilt that the sterile "Dougs" carry. The wonder is that Bill and Carol have, in fact, "held out" as long as they have!

Doug and Jane have taken the easy way out by focusing all their energies on the work of the local congregation. They have retreated to the safe, insular life of fellowship with like-minded people.

This is not to suggest that they should disengage themselves from the local assembly . . . not at all! Rather, they should broaden their horizon to see before them the more total community-wide ministry. We admit that such a ministry has a high level of risk involved in it. There is much room for misunderstanding (as Bill suffers), and there may even be moments when it is "necessary" for the brothers to help him "clean up his act a bit" because he has gone too far.

The personal risk suggested here is precisely the risk that organizations like Young Life Campaign and the Billy Graham Evangelistic Association have taken. They, as well as anyone in the body of Christ, understand what is involved in community penetration . . . and have suffered much misunderstanding and criticism as a result.

In a sense, Bill and Doug have much in common. Both are misunderstood by their peer group in the local assembly; Bill for his involvement with the world and Doug for his lack of involvement in the world. Their lives need not be a study of contrast, but harmony. Bill needs Doug. Doug needs Bill. Ideally, they can wonderfully complement each other.

## Complementing Ministries

First, how can Doug, the ineffective witness, help Bill? How do you keep a Bill growing and on proper course in the ministry while, at the same time, help him maintain his valuable contact with the world—which is what the Christian ministry is designed to reach?

Bill needs Doug's *support,* for Doug also under-stands the milieu of the marketplace. Day after day he, too, enters the same tough arena in which Bill functions.

Another key is Doug's *maturity and depth in the Word.* If Doug and Bill functioned together in a support group where Bill could gain encourage-ment and perspective from Doug, the risks would be minimized and the ministry maximized.

Second, how can Bill, the tobacco executive, help Doug? Risk-taking is a fearful thing. It is not easy for a man who has spent most of his life in the Christian ghetto to suddenly break out and become involved in the lives of publicans and sinners. Bill's *pacesetting* would be an encouragement and incentive to Doug. The local congregations are full of Dougs who need to see the model of the free and accepting way Bill relates to the non-Christian. In-stead of stifling Bill, Doug should encourage and emulate him.

Third, what part can the local congregation play in the lives of both men?

They can play a strategic role. The pastor must not see his role as channeling and controlling *all the energies* of these men in the direction of the assembly's program. His job, rather, is to equip these men for the work of the ministry in their specific arenas. They are disciples, not sheep. They need more than food; they need to be ably equipped!

When the "Bills" maintain habits that are objec-tionable to the fellowship, the pastor should not be intimidated. Instead, in an accepting manner, he must objectively ask himself:

1) Are the habits biblically wrong? The believer is free to maintain any habit as long as the Bible and the Holy Spirit do not check him.

2) Does Bill see the habits as wrong? The pastor and members of the assembly must distinguish between perception and rebellion on Bill's part. Some individuals are nonconformists, not because they are resisting the truth, but simply because they don't see the truth. Only the Holy Spirit dispenses the fruits of the Spirit. The congregation must be patient and allow Bill to learn those lessons that only the living God can teach.

Proverbs 27:17 says, "As iron sharpens iron, so one man sharpens another." Bill and Doug are cut out of different cloth. This is the genius of what God is doing in the world today. Would to God that they have a healthy appreciation for one another—"Until we all reach unity in the faith and in the knowledge of the Son of God and become mature, attaining to the whole measure of the fullness of Christ" (Eph. 4:13).

### FOR DISCUSSION

1. Which man, Doug or Bill, are you most like? Why?

2. What steps are you taking (or can you take) to obtain more balance in your life?

3. Do you know any "Dougs" or "Bills" you can help? How would you go about doing this?

4. List some possible "Dougs" or "Bills" who can help you.

# CHAPTER 4

# FIVE BASIC CHARACTERISTICS OF FUNCTIONING LAYMEN

There is a story told of Jesus being met at heaven's gate by Gabriel, the archangel. Gabriel asked, "Lord, where have You been?"

"On earth, Gabriel, to die for the sins of the world."

"That is wonderful, Lord, but how is the world to hear of this great thing You have done?"

"I took three years to train twelve men. They have been commissioned with the task."

"But, Lord," protested Gabriel, "What if they fail? What other plan do You have?"

"Gabriel, I have no other plan."

These twelve men to whom Jesus entrusted the job of propagating the good news were all business and professional men—as were the men like Barnabas, Paul, and Luke who served Him later. They all used their vocation as part of the overall arena in which they functioned as God's men. Peter continued to fish after he met Christ, but he didn't give his life in exchange for fish. Paul made tents for a living, but his goal in life was not to become the largest tent manufacturer in the Roman empire.

As a man seeks to maintain proper priorities, what is to be the balance? As he seeks to penetrate his sphere of influence with the living Christ, what should characterize his ministry?

A group of business and professional men recently gathered in Denver, Colorado, to ask themselves that very question. It wasn't an attempt to define an exhaustive set of priorities in life. Rather, they sought to identify the key characteristics seen in the lives of people God uses. Five such characteristics of functioning laymen in the ministry were listed. But, first, what do we mean by "ministry"?

## A Definition of Ministry

There is much ambiguity surrounding the whole concept of the ministry. What is it? What does it entail? For example, are you doing the ministry if you "give a cold cup of water to the thirsty"? Does involvement in helping the poor and the distressed constitute doing the ministry? If so, how does this differ from similar involvements on the part of non-Christians? A concerned Buddhist or Moslem can emulate the ministry in this sense.

Ministry, in order for it to be distinctively serving the gospel of Christ, must have at least two ingredients:

MOTIVE. The aim or goal of ministry activities *is to bring people into a relationship with Jesus Christ and to encourage the deepening of that relationship where it already exists.* The cup of cold water is in "Jesus' name." The driving force behind all that is done is motivated by the commitment to Christ and a desire to share Him with others.

METHOD. Jesus said, "All men will know that you are my disciples if you love one another" (John 13:35). Ministry is done with the loving concern of Jesus Himself. Not only is it done in His name, but also in His way.

### Five Essential Characteristics

A certain risk is involved in listing indispensable ingredients in the life of a functioning believer. "Who says they are essential?" is the natural response to such assertions. Hopefully, as they are discussed, the fact that they are essential will be "self evident"—obvious that they are irreducible minimums from a biblical perspective.

This is not to suggest they are exhaustive. For example, there has been no effort to emphasize the importance of the family, and yet all would agree that this is an important priority. When the men met in Denver to discuss these characteristics, they sought to narrow their attention to just those aspects that deal *directly with ministry,* realizing, for example, that many of them are also applicable to the family.

Another risk in compiling this list is the aspect of quality. Who is to say when a person is effectively functioning in these areas? What is the standard of evaluation? Compared to what? No one can answer these questions for another. There are too many variables in each individual's life for a uniform standard of performance. A person's spiritual age, maturity, gifts, abilities, perception of God's will for his life—all contribute to making the question of performance relative.

Each must ask the Lord what He would have him do. God's will for each believer, within the biblical parameters, is personal and individual. As a layman seeks to help another maximize his potential for Christ, he cannot tell him what he must do in these five categories; but he simply helps him, in any way he can, gain proficiency in these areas.

The five categories themselves are self-evident from the Scriptures. An individual will function effectively to the degree that his "filter" or "grid" affirms that these are biblical and to the degree that he is submissive to God's will. The disciple's job is not to coerce another into conformity with what he thinks the other ought to do, but rather to help him in any way he can to be and do what the other feels God wants him to be and do. We will now discuss the five characteristics you and every disciple must have and practice.

## One: Depth in Your Spiritual Life

This must be central. You must know God and follow Him as life's number one priority. This is utterly essential to everything else this book states.

Are you walking with Jesus? Are you feeding your own soul through the Word and prayer? Are you walking in obedience to the known will of God? Is your fellowship with the Savior sweet and intimate?

As you take spiritual inventory and answer these questions, where do you begin? The following are some suggested guideposts:

WORD: As you fellowship with God, two-way conversation is imperative. Time spent in the Bible affords you the opportunity to listen to God. There are five ways to do this:

1. *Hear.* Even though you are a disciple you are also a sheep. You need some feeding from your local pastor. You should have a satisfactory relationship with your local congregation. This is the ideal place to hear the exposition of the Scriptures, but it is usually not sufficient in and of itself. Tapes, radio, television, conferences, seminars are also good ways to augment your scriptural intake. When listening to the Word, take notes. This will help both with concentration and retention.

2. *Read.* A good reading program is helpful in giving a panoramic view of the Bible, as well as a good way to spend devotional time with the Lord. *Walk Thru The Bible* is an outstanding program.

44

(Information on this program can be obtained from: Walk Thru The Bible Ministries, Inc., 603 Peachtree St., N.E., Atlanta, GA 30308).

3. *Study.* Much is available in Bible study methodology. For group study, look into Bible Study Fellowship. It is a comprehensive investigation of the whole Bible. The study is rigorous and demanding, but well worth the effort. Their address is: Bible Study Fellowship, 19001 Blanco Road, San Antonio, TX 78258.

4. *Memorize.* One of the best introductions to Scripture memory is the *Topical Memory System,* published by The Navigators. It is available in several translations and teaches *how* to memorize the Word as well as gives key verses, by topics, which are important for Christian living. Write: The Navigators, P.O. Box 6000, Colorado Springs, Colorado 80934.

The most complete single arming of the man of God to do the work of God is through the Word of God. Second Timothy 3:16–17 says, "All Scripture is God-breathed and is useful for teaching, rebuking, correcting and training in righteousness, so that the man of God may be thoroughly equipped for every good work."

*PRAYER:* This is the other half of the two-way conversation. An excellent motivational booklet on the subject is E.M. Bounds' *Power Through Prayer,* (Zondervan). Motivation is essential, for prayer does not come easy for the average person. For private praying, one may wish to consider:

1. *Prayer pages.* These enable you to develop a system for remembering the people you pray for regularly. Some will be prayed for daily—others weekly. Make one page for the daily requests, such as the family, uncommitted relatives and friends, and a page for each day of the week for other needs. Be sure to leave room to record *answers* to personal requests.

2. *Prayer partners.* It is often more easy to concentrate if you pray with someone else. The married disciple should pray daily with his wife, or she with her husband, especially for those needs that are common to both of them. Select a prayer partner from your "core fellowship" of close Christian brothers and sisters and commit your self to a regular time of protracted prayer with your partner. Prayer is the ministry. God moves in the lives of people in answer to prayer!

*THANKSGIVING:* "Depth in the personal life" is impossible without having a thankful heart. In Romans 1, Paul charts the downward spiral of our depravity. Verse 21 shows that a root cause of this downfall is a thankless heart: "For although they knew God, they neither glorified him as God nor gave thanks to him, but their thinking became futile and their foolish hearts were darkened."

The natural person says, "Life owes me more than I have. I deserve a better deal." Reflect for a moment about how wonderful God is. An American living in the United States is within the top 10% of all the people of the world as far as enjoying creature comforts. If the disciple wishes to function as God's man, a basic requisite is a thankful heart.

*SURRENDER:* Surrender is a natural response when you begin to grow in the realization of the greatness of God. When Saul of Tarsus met Jesus Christ on the road to Damascus, he had but two questions: "Who are You, Lord?" and "What do You want me to do?" These questions are indicative of a heart submitted to God.

"Show me who You are and tell me what You want me to do." The more clearly you see the character of God, the more eager you are to obey Him. This is why surrender is one of the great indications of where you are in your walk with God. Surrender is indispensable for the person who wants a slice of the action in God's program in history. It is foundational in knowing God's will for your life. The disciple who aspires to dwell in the high and holy habitations of God must have a contrite and humble spirit:

> For this is what the high and lofty One says—he who lives forever, whose name is holy: "I live in a high and holy place, but also with him who is contrite and lowly in spirit, to revive the spirit of the lowly and to revive the heart of the contrite (Isa. 57:15).

The depth of your walk with God will determine the quality of all your relationships. How you relate to your spouse, children, employer / employees, pastor, and friends are all a by-product of your relationship with God. So consistently does this hold true that Solomon advises, "When a man's ways are pleasing to the LORD, he makes even his enemies live at peace with him" (Prov. 16:7).

## Two: Penetrating the Uncommitted

When Peter wrote his first letter he addressed it to the "aliens" scattered throughout the various provinces of the Roman empire. You as a believer are an "alien." Made new in Jesus Christ, you are no longer part of the world system. You live in it, but refuse to sell your soul to it. Day in and out, you rub shoulders with people enslaved by the system. The *worth of the individual* is a foreign concept to them because their lives have never been touched by the One in whose image they were created.

Bridging the gulf between this imprisonment of the human spirit and the liberation available in Christ is the challenge to you as you labor in the marketplace. You are to model the character and fragrance of Christ before a hostile world and this contrasting lifestyle evokes a response from the non-Christian. Sometimes that response is animosity as he lashes out at that which he cannot understand. Other times it asks probing questions seeking to identify the difference. In either case, Peter says, "Always be prepared to give an answer to everyone who asks you to give the reason for the hope that you have" (1 Peter 3:15).

Personal Bible study and prayer will help prepare you to give your "answer." There are also a number of ministry vehicles available to supplement personal witness. It is impossible to list all of them, but the following are representative:

1. *Christian Business Men's Committee.* In many cities businessmen have banded together with the help of this organization to help one another reach uncommitted business associates. Usually at a meal where the follower of Christ invites his friend, an out-of-town guest (always a layman) tells his story of how he met Christ and the difference it has made in his family and business. The meeting closes with a tastefully presented opportunity to respond to the claims of Christ. For those who do not have a Christian Business Men's Committee locally, but feel it might meet a need, write P.O. Box 3380, Chattanooga, Tennessee 37404.

2. *Search Ministries.* The approach here is for believers to invite their non-Christian friends to an evening meeting in someone's home. The meeting is advertised as a "religious discussion" where anyone can ask questions on any subject dealing with religion. A trained discussion group leader chairs the meeting and simply functions as a sounding board and referee. Four sessions are held, usually once a week, then the meetings end. It becomes readily apparent who the people are who are asking honest questions. Appointments are made with them individually, and the gospel is presented at that time. Write: P.O. Box 31268, Dallas, Texas 75231.

3. *Outreach Dinners.* A couple invite a group of nonbelievers to their home for a dinner and an opportunity to hear a guest speaker. Formal invitations are sent requiring an RSVP. On the invitation it is clearly stated that "religion" is involved. Many who receive these invitations are not even known by the host couple. Still, approximately 25% seem to respond. An invitation to receive Christ is given at the close of the dinner meeting. If such an approach strikes a responsive chord, write: Executive Ministries, P.O. Box 1091, Bryn Mawr, PA 19010.

## Three: Discipling

The nurture and care of God's people is extremely important to Him. It is one of the staggering truths of the Scriptures that the care of His people has been entrusted to His servants. Involvement in God's program entails the care and feeding of His sheep (as explained in chapter 2).

Disciples, who have fulfilled further obligations of Christ, can make other disciples. Such care is costly, for it requires an in-depth involvement in the lives of people. Since few are willing to pay the price, this adds to the burden of those who are making disciples.

Writing to the Thessalonians, Paul said, "We loved you so much that we were delighted to share with you not only the gospel of God but out lives as well, because you had become so dear to us" (1 Thess. 2:8). It wasn't just a message that Paul imparted, it was his very life.

This does not mean that you as a disciple are

responsible to meet *all* the needs in the life of another. No one person can do this, for no one person has all the gifts. This is where "body life" comes into play.

As a parent I am not responsible for meeting all the needs of my children. If my son breaks his arm, I don't set it. But I am responsible for seeing that the needs of my children are met. I will take him to a doctor and have him set the arm. The same principle applies to discipling. Others in Christ's body will help meet the needs of those whom you are seeking to influence.

As you reflect on your inadequacies, it may seem awesome that you can assume the responsibility for others. Here is where you often may feel this is a job for the "professional." A word of encouragement to you: as the necessary credentials for being a good father are *concern coupled with common sense,* so it is with discipling. The whole subject of discipling is treated more fully in *Disciples Are Made Not Born,* by Walter Henrichsen, published by Victor Books.

### Four: Core Fellowship

Solomon said, in Ecclesiastes 4:9–10, "Two are better than one, because they have a good return for their work: If one falls down, his friend can help him up. But pity the man who falls and has no one to help him up!" People are created to need one another. The benefits of a "core fellowship" are *support, objectivity of counsel,* and *accountability.* Everyone needs the support of others.

1. *Support.* The ministry to which God has called you will not go unchallenged. Many of you may feel that your efforts for Christ will be legitimate *only* as part of and under the control of the institutional religious groups. Therefore, the prayer and encouragement of a band of like-minded brothers are crucial.

2. *Objectivity of counsel.* Every person needs others in whom he can confide, talk through problems and needs with, to explore options, and to get advice.

3. *Accountability.* Hebrews 13:17 says, "Obey your leaders and submit to their authority. They keep watch over you as men who must give an account." In an antiauthoritarian age most people shun the concept of accountability. Discipline as outlined in Matthew 18:15–17 is virtually unknown in most fellowships. Yet it is one of the richest heritages Christianity has—brothers and sisters who love one another so much that they tell it like it is.

If you are not functioning in a small fellowship (and it may not be larger than three or four), you can ask God to lead you to those who will enter into a covenant of this kind with you. David and Jonathan developed this kind of relationship (1 Sam. 18). It doesn't need to be structured. Honesty and openness are important; and this requires a willingness for self-disclosure. As love and acceptance are communicated, this will become increasingly easy.

## Five: Vision

Dawson Trotman, founder of The Navigators, stressed having bifocal vision. This is the ability to see clearly what God wants you to do where you are, while at the same time having an appreciation for what He is doing in and through the rest of the body of Christ.

It is easy to fall into one of two extremes. Some disciples are so involved in *their* ministry they have little time or appreciation for what is happening elsewhere in the work of Christ. Conversely, some are so active traveling to and becoming involved in what God is doing elsewhere that they have no time to develop a ministry of their own. You must not fall into an either-or trap. You should seek to maintain a balance.

"Lord, give me a clear picture of what You are doing in the world and the part You want me to play in it," is the heart cry of the person with vision. "Show me Your greatness and give me a slice of the action."

To do this will require effort. You will need to ask the Lord to give you an appreciation for the ministries of others and spend the effort to get to know more about them. You will need to be single-minded in regard to God's will for your life, and not be small in your thinking. The program of God is vast. He refuses to be restricted by organizational policies and creeds.

Bob Pierce, founder of World Vision, prayed, "Lord, break my heart with the things that break Your heart."

Be a man of *vision*.

## Conclusion

We are cautioned in Matthew 6:24, "No one can serve two masters. Either he will hate the one and love the other, or he will be devoted to the one and despise the other. You cannot serve both God and Money." The temptation to serve two masters seems to be uniquely strong for the follower of Christ who is in business. He wants to serve God, yet he needs a certain recognition from the world to know that his gifts and capacities are being adequately used in his profession. It is as though he uses two score cards.

Most men are not allowed to keep score by both systems. Usually the Lord forces a confrontation, and the man must choose. For some this comes when advancement in the corporation is offered, for others with the temptation of great financial gain, and even others with the reaching of certain, long-awaited goals. A choice inevitably must be made: God or recognition. God or advancement. God or money. If you try to serve *both*, God always loses. And you lose a more ultimate goal.

There is a price to pay for being God's man or woman. It begins by serving only one master.

### FOR DISCUSSION

1. What is a Christian ministry? Does your ministry have these characteristics?

2. How do you rate in the five essential characteristics? Where are you strongest? Where weakest? Do you know how to get help where you are weak? Do you know how to help others with your strengths?

3. What, as a result of this chapter, will you do to grow?

4. Do you have some like-minded brothers to whom you are accountable and who are accountable to you?

5. Are you trying to serve God and money? What would be a more proper balance in your life in this regard?

# CHAPTER 5

# HOW TO BE FULLY EQUIPPED

*The disciple must have a thorough, comprehensive view of the Scriptures. If he is going to minister for Him, it is imperative that he be fully equipped.*

Paul had invested three years of his life in the city of Ephesus. The ministry was fruitful, resulting in the formation of a virile local congregation. Some of the flock grew from sheep into disciples. Paul appointed elders from among these maturing disciples. Then he left Ephesus to continue on his third missionary journey.

Months later, he returned to the coast of Miletus.

He summoned the Ephesian elders to visit him. He somehow sensed this would be the last time they would be together. As he reviewed his ministry in their lives, he said, "Wherefore I take you to record this day, that I am pure from the blood of all men. For I have not shunned to declare unto you all the counsel of God" (Acts 20:26–27 KJV).

What an awe-inspiring statement! Seeking to prepare them for the day when "grievous wolves" would come among them to trouble them, he had communicated the entire "counsel" of God. Is it reasonable to assume that Paul had told everything? If not, he had at least given them exposure to the entire spectrum of truth in the Old Testament, plus what the Holy Spirit had given him in what would become the New Testament.

*What person today would claim to have imparted the entire counsel of God?* Perhaps some of the great Bible expositors have done so, but to turn this question around: *To what degree have lay people been exposed to the whole counsel of God—having a thorough, comprehensive view of the Scriptures?*

## The Need

The theme of this book is that God is on schedule in the building of His church . . . that His method is disciples who are able to function to His glory in the context of the work-a-day world . . . and that lay men and women, not institutions, are central to the program of God.

Any imbalances in your life as a lay person will be adjusted only as you avail yourself of and become obedient to the whole counsel of God. It is as you expose yourself to the entire revelation of God that you become adequately and accurately transformed into the image of His Son. This in turn equips you to be His ambassador in the marketplace.

This is no easy task, for it is rare even for the seminary graduate to have been adequately exposed to the whole Bible, enabling him to be at home in all its various parts. The depths of Scripture to be plumbed are so great that in a lifetime of preaching and teaching a person can scarcely scratch the surface. Many therefore avoid, with apparent justification, those portions to which he or she is least attracted. But this is not as it should be!

If there are portions of the Scriptures with which you are not familiar or which make you feel uncomfortable, you should hasten to hear what fresh truths in those areas the Holy Spirit will have you learn. It would be well for you to analyze your biblical intake in light of the "whole counsel of God" and begin learning in those areas you have been neglecting.

To assist you in having a total biblical view, here is a broad classification of Scripture into five divisions:

## Classification of Scripture

1. New Testament history or narrative: Matthew, Mark, Luke, John, and the Acts of the Apostles.
2. New Testament letters of instruction to the first-century churches and their leaders: Ro-

mans through Jude. These are the writings of
Paul, Peter, John, James, and Jude.
3. Devotional literature or records of the com-
   munications between God and many of His
   choice Old Testament servants: Job, Psalms,
   Proverbs, Ecclesiastes, and Solomon's Song
   of Songs.
4. Old Testament history of God's dealings with
   His people Israel: Genesis through Esther.
5. Old Testament prophets Isaiah through
   Malachi, and the New Testament book,
   Revelation: preaching and warning to the
   nation Israel through a whole new class of
   servants of God after the moral decline of the
   kings and priests.

There are significant overlaps in this broad out-
line. For example, much devotional literature is
scattered throughout the entire Bible. Prophetic
literature is found in Deuteronomy as well as in
the gospels, and there is also instructional material
in the gospels.

These broad categories can, however, serve as a
test to see where each disciple stands in his exposure to the "whole counsel" and where correction
is needed. There are some generally predictable
results that accrue from a neglect of any of these
categories. Using broad brush strokes, here is a
description of each of these five categories:

## Category 1—The Gospels and Acts

Most preaching in the usual evangelical church
will concern itself with those passages of Scripture
falling within Categories 1 & 2 but, as between

these categories, a balance is necessary. When there is a preoccupation with the first five books in the New Testament, accompanied by a neglect of the epistles, relatively unstructured theological patterns emerge. The teachings of Christ are multipurposed. He addresses Himself to the disciples, to the Jewish multitude, the hostile Jewish leaders, the ruling representatives of the Roman Empire, and to an occasional Gentile, and each group has special needs to be dealt with effectively.

The recorded events and teachings are chosen by the writers under the direction of the Holy Spirit for all the purposes of His ministry to be revealed, and to assume indiscriminately that the message arising out of every encounter recorded in the gospel accounts was directed with equal weight and with the same application to all the hearers is unrealistic. Most obviously it insinuates that the writers of the New Testament epistles either did not understand the teachings of Jesus or were disobedient in applying it in their own ministries. It should be safely assumed that models of obedience will be seen in the epistles and that the New Testament writers in their instructions and exhortations were completely consistent with the teachings and examples of Jesus.

An opposite presumption manifests itself in many current writings, and an example is Richard Quebedeaux's volume, *The Young Evangelicals.* We suggest that if he had tested in advance his conclusions from the teachings of Jesus by the response of the apostles and the later writers of the New Testament, he would not have had to do so much rethinking and readjustment in his later book, *The Worldly Evangelicals.*

A controversial evangelical magazine of noble purpose, *Sojourners,* makes infrequent use of the epistles. It uses the gospel accounts almost exclusively, with a few passages from the prophets, to exhort its readers to social action, antinuclear activity, or other emphases that its editors may select from time to time. Since the New Testament writers do not have the same emphasis, one is lead to believe that the apostles failed to meet the litmus test that the editors of *Sojourners* apply as their standard for determining the reality of one's Christian life.

The charismatic movement relies on the four gospel accounts, but also draws disproportionately on the accounts of the experiences of the early church provided in the Acts of the Apostles. This is not to suggest that it is simple to bring into harmony all of the gospel accounts, the Book of Acts, and the various epistles. The evangelical assumption that they all make up a significant portion of the whole counsel makes that, however, a practical goal to strive for.

### Category 2—The New Testament Epistles

When the emphasis of teaching in a given assembly or denomination places an undue emphasis on the New Testament letters without being balanced with the teachings of the gospel accounts, the result can be cold and rigid, systematic thinking. Truth tends to be seen as propositional, lending itself to a very satisfying system, and any deviation that is apt to challenge the logic of that system is viewed with great suspicion. These teachers have their roots deeply in both the Reformed and the dispensational traditions and confess that both of these systems encourage this emphasis.

Sometimes it seems that the whole of Bible interpretation is one large crossword puzzle, the purpose of which is to fill all of the blocks and use up all of the definitions and discover exactly the right words to complete the pattern. This becomes an end in itself and a grid through which all new offering of Truth is to be screened. It sometimes seems that the successful completion of the puzzle, rightfully accounting for all the truth in sight, is an end in itself. It is easy at this point to forget that in God's purposes the provision of truth is to produce godly living and obedience to Him, and without that we become "a noisy gong or a clanging cymbal." The Bible in the New Testament cautions against this with severe warnings to "do the deeds you did at first," and the path to that end is contact with the living Christ in the gospel accounts.

### Category 3—Devotional Literature

This is the literature of the mystic. It is the language of prayer itself. In it God gives you the words, phrases, concepts, and insights with which to worship Him better.

Worship originates from daily life, so it should be part of daily life. Whatever your vocation or calling in life, this category gives wisdom to live daily to His glory. The devotional life is greatly enhanced by consistent contact with these books.

Committed Christians through the centuries have memorized portions of this literature and found them to be immensely helpful in their walk with the Lord.

### Category 4—Old Testament History

Most of the New Testament was written by Jews to Jews; therefore, most of the chapters have some reference to God's dealing with His people in the Old Testament. The Book of Hebrews assumes a thorough knowledge of the first five books of the Bible. Paul, a Jewish scholar, quotes profusely from the Old Testament in Romans and Galatians.

Since the Christian life usually starts in the New Testament, and since the New Testament draws so heavily from the Old Testament, one would think that most believers would quickly begin studying portions of the Old. Unfortunately, this is not always true. Some never make any significant contact with the first thirty-nine books of the Bible.

Paul, in his first letter to the Corinthians, drew from an experience in Israel's history to teach an important truth disciples are to live by today. Here is what he says about Old Testament history:

Now these things occurred as examples, to keep us from setting our hearts on evil things as they did (1 Cor. 10:6).

Not only is an understanding of the Old Testament necessary for a proper grasp of the New Testament, but the former provides a source of rich application for the Christian's life. More than seventy-five times the New Testament makes reference to Abraham to show how he acted out the nuances of a life of faith—which Christians, in turn, are to emulate!

Chapter 11 of Hebrews is a roll call of God's "greats." All but one were laymen. Samuel was the exception, and he is only given honorable mention. For example, the reader is told to consider the actions of such a person as a harlot, Rahab. She *acted* on her beliefs. This is a lesson for you as a disciple today.

A proper concept of God implies an understanding of *all* He has said. Until the historical books of the Old Testament begin to dynamically live within you—until you walk with God vicariously through the lives of those men of old, learning why He exalted some and rejected others—your view of God will remain greatly limited.

## Category 5—Prophetic Books

This is generally the last portion of the Bible that God's people begin to study. Many never do. In fact, it is the most neglected source of Bible teaching and preaching of our day.

God selected His prophets from the various tribes of the nations of Israel. There were sixteen writing prophets, and of this group Zechariah and Ezekiel were from priestly origin. Isaiah and Daniel were probably from noble and high ranking families. The remaining twelve have very obscure geneologies, and nothing is known about the background of some of them.

The problem often is that the larger context of the prophetic messages is ignored in favor of selected warnings about sin. With this treatment the prophets appear to be very grim and judgmental in their attitudes. As basic life relationships deteriorate, messages are proclaimed from the pulpit on statements such as:

"For I hate divorce"—Malachi;
"Reprove the ruthless"—Isaiah;
"Plead for the widow"—Isaiah.

It is submitted that there is a larger message that is prominent throughout all of the prophetic books and to ignore this, making them simply a repository of convenient proof texts, is to miss the perspective and dynamic that the Holy Spirit would have us receive from this portion of His Word. In fact, the only way correction will occur in the course of such sins is to dwell on the graciousness of God. Our human relationships are in order in direct proportion to how well our relationship to a gracious God is in order.

While all the prophets deal with the current sins and shortcomings of the nation of Israel prevalent during the day in which each of them wrote, there is persistent and continuous praise to the God who is and will be faithful to His people Israel. Because the theologians of our day are in disagreement concerning the manifestation of this commitment on God's part, they tend to avoid these passages in general or use them only in a very selective manner. While it is important to hear the warnings of the prophets it must be seen in the context of the gracious commitment that God has made to His people, commencing with the patriarchs, and to

His sovereign commitment for the fulfillment of those promises. Israel's basic failure is the same as our continuing failure, that is to "grow in grace." We, like they, become presumptuous in our daily lives, becoming insensitive to our own propensity to sin and indifference.

The continuous thread through all the prophets is the unifying theme of grace, not judgment. The prophet Jeremiah in the midst of his lamentation over the city of Jerusalem sings, "Great Is Thy faithfulness." No matter how intense the judgment of God at any moment in the Old Testament the prophets unanimously attest that God's promises to Israel are irrevocable. This awareness of God's sovereign commitment to His people is necessary for an adequate perspective of what He is doing at any moment in history. This larger view of God's overall strategy is given to us so that we can see the relevance of the day-to-day tasks we must perform in our lives.

> Everything is appropriate in its own time. But though God has planted eternity in the hearts of men, even so, man cannot see the whole scope of God's work from beginning to end. (Eccl. 3:11 Living Bible)

One word of warning in connection with the whole counsel of God. It is a good idea to read and study the Bible with a constant reminder of its central message. Donald Grey Barnhouse insisted that the message of the Bible could be summarized as "God's perfect remedy for man's complete ruin."

From the beginning of Genesis to the end of Revelation, it reveals the grace of God "fleshed out" in illustrations.

## Conclusion

God is at work in the lives of people in a way unparalleled in contemporary times. Possibly this age will herald His second coming.

Therefore, the laity have an increased burden to shepherd and disciple men and women to move from "darkness to light, from the power of Satan to God." Man reproduces after his own kind. If he is stunted and deficient in his understanding of God as He has revealed Himself in the totality of Scripture, so will be those in whose lives he invests time. To raise up men and women of God he needs to be a man or woman who knows the whole Book.

"'The harvest is plentiful but the workers are few'" (Matt. 9:37). Disciples who qualify for the harvest must know and impart the whole counsel of God.

### FOR DISCUSSION

1. Of the five classes of Scripture, where are you the strongest? The weakest? How will you balance this? What specific help do you need to balance this?

2. Establish, this week, a study program to become more balanced.

3. What are you currently doing to help others develop a balanced understanding of the Scriptures? What changes do you feel God would have you make as you help others?

# PART TWO

# LAYMEN AND THE CHURCH

*Jesus said, "For where two or three come together in my name, there am I with them."*

# CHAPTER 6

# THE OLD TESTAMENT DEVELOPMENT OF THE LAYMEN'S MINISTRY

*To have an accurate and objective view of the church, it is imperative that you have a clear understanding of God's program in history and what He is doing in the world today. Unfortunately, a proper perspective of what God is doing does not mean you will automatically have an accurate and objective view of the organized church.*

The layman is in the middle of God's program throughout history. It started right at the beginning . . .

## Each Man Was His Own Priest

In Genesis 4:3–5 both Cain and Abel functioned in the capacity of priest in that each was responsible for his own offering to God.

Genesis has many accounts of each man acting as his own priest. Genesis 8:20 says, "Then Noah built an altar to the LORD and, taking some of all the clean animals and clean birds, he sacrificed burnt offerings on it."

Again and again, Abraham offered sacrifices to God, as did his sons and grandsons. Thus, originally in man's relations with God, every individual functioned as his own priest before God with no particular location established for sacrificing and with no intermediary between him and God.

## The First "Professional" Priests

Exodus is the story of God's bringing His people, Israel, out of Egypt into the promised land of Canaan. The principle architect of this "exodus" or "mass departure" was Moses.

It was during this journey that the "Mt. Sinai experience" occurred, which indicated *a major change in God's dealing with man.* When Moses went up to the mountain to receive a list of rules and regulations (the Law) for the newly freed nation, God also gave him instructions to form a "professional priesthood." Now each layman would no longer be his own priest ... the individual could no longer take his sacrifices directly to God.

72

From this point on, each Israelite had to bring his offering to a specific place and allow a Levite to go before God on his behalf. (God had indicated that the members of one of the twelve tribes, Levi, were to be given the function of priests—thus, the *Levitical* order).

The Book of Hebrews gives two reasons why God centralized the priesthood under the Levites:

1. *To show the inadequacy of man's efforts to atone for sin.* Hebrews 10:1–4 says, "The law is only a shadow of the good things that are coming—not the realities themselves. For this reason it can never, by the same sacrifices repeated endlessly year after year, make perfect those who draw near to worship. If it could, would they not have stopped being offered? For the worshipers would have been cleansed once for all, and would no longer have felt guilty for their sins. But those sacrifices are an annual reminder of sins, because it is impossible for the blood of bulls and goats to take away sins."

The repetition of those sacrifices at that one locality was a vivid reminder of man's futile efforts to make appeasement for his own sins.

2. *To give a picture of God's solution to man's problem.* Note in Hebrews 9:9, 23, 24 and 10:1 the use of words like "illustration," "copy," and "shadow." This is what the sacrificial system, under the Levitical order, was to the cross—a preview of coming attractions. Though only a shadow, these sacrifices pointed to God's solution

for man's sin in Jesus Christ—which, again, as the next chapter will show, was another change in the way God deals with man.

## FOR DISCUSSION

1. Do you understand the concept "each man is his own priest"? Explain it in your own words.

# CHAPTER 7

# THE NEW TESTAMENT DEVELOPMENT OF THE LAYMEN'S MINISTRY

*To view the organized church run by the professionals as the sole legitimate expression of God's ministry is to regress to the Old Testament Levitical perspective.*

## The Professional Priesthood Ends With Christ's Death

The crucifixion ended the Levitical order.

Matthew's account of the crucifixion records the splitting of the veil that separated the Holy of Holies from the rest of the temple. Occurring at the moment of Christ's death, this destruction of the veil heralded the end of the Levitical order. (Previously, only the high priest could go into the Holy of Holies and directly confront God).

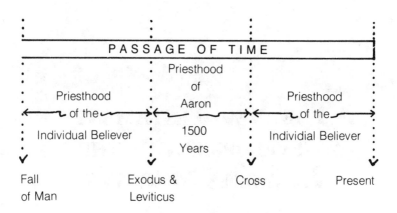

ILLUSTRATION 1

But now, as the author of Hebrews, who is writing to Jewish believers, says, "Let us then approach the throne of grace with confidence, so that we may receive mercy and find grace to help us in our time of need" (4:16).

Both Peter and John declare that *all believers are priests*. First Peter 2:9 says, "But you are a chosen people, a royal priesthood. . . ." Revelation 1:6 says, ". . . and has made us to be a kingdom and priests to serve his God and Father—to him be glory and power for ever and ever!"

Put into historical perspective, the priesthood concept (see Illustration #1) would look like this: for the first several thousand years of mankind's history as recorded in the Bible, each man was responsible for functioning as a priest before God. Then, for approximately 1500 years, the time between Moses and when Christ appeared on earth, the priesthood of the professional existed. From the death of Christ until He returns again, we have reverted to the pre-Sinai days of the priesthood of the believer.

Each believer is free to represent himself to God and to represent God to those who as yet have not encountered Christ. (This is not to suggest there are no *offices* in the New Testament. There are elders, deacons, apostles, etc. In the multiplicity of offices, however, there is no priesthood apart from the priesthood of the believer. *No office can usurp from the believer his role and right to function as God's priest.*)

This right of individual priesthood became the dynamic of the New Testament Church. Each believer viewed himself as a priest of God to a broken world. Each felt he had the right and responsibility to function in the office of the priesthood. During those embryonic days of the church, *no distinction was made between the laity and the professional.*

Paul explains this doctrine in Ephesians 4: 11–13:

> It was he who gave some to be apostles, some to be prophets, some to be evangelists, and some to be pastors and teachers, to prepare God's people for works of service, so that the body of Christ may be built up until we all reach unity in the faith and in the knowledge of the Son of God and become ma-

ture, attaining to the whole measure of the fullness of Christ.

The vocational Christian workers mentioned in verse 11 are charged with the task of equipping the saints (the laity) so that the laity will be able to do the work of the ministry (verse 12). As the saints do the work of the ministry, the church is edified.

The New Testament concept of the ministry could be analogous to a large pond into which the Holy Spirit scatters believers here and about like tossing pebbles. As each believer hits his particular sphere of influence, the impact makes concentric circles that move out and eventually overlap with the circles of influence of other believer "pebbles." Thus, the whole pond is "covered."

It is unfortunate that many believers today view the ministry primarily as the job of the pastor. The pastor is like a giant boulder thrown into the community. The huge wave he makes upon impact is supposed to cover the pond. This is a critical contrast to the each-believer-a-pebble (each-believer-a-priest) concept!

Acts 8:5-38 is a good example of a layman ministering in the marketplace. Philip (a lay deacon, not one of the apostles) ministered the Word in the city of Samaria. Many responded to the Good News and were baptized by him. Later, he led an Ethiopian to Christ in Gaza and baptized him.

## The Reinstitution of the Levitical Order

As the first century ended, an extrabiblical word was introduced into the church: clergy. With the spread of the gospel came growth, and with growth came the desire to establish a "full-time professional clergy" to manage and control the growing church.

Thus, a distinction between "laity" and "professional" began. Christianity has been plagued with it ever since. More and more the church began to structure itself on the basis of the former Levitical order, *rather than on the purely New Testament idea of "each man is a priest" perspective.*

The theological justification for going back to the old idea was the conviction that the church was the "new Israel." All the promises God had made to the Jews through the prophets would find their fulfillment in the church. Therefore, it was only natural to also look to the Old Testament for the form, now that the function was already embraced. That form was the Levitical priesthood.

The change was slow and evolutionary, but pastors gradually came to be called "priests" and the believers "laity." The communion table became an altar and the elements a sacrifice. People were discouraged from reading and interpreting the Bible on their own. It had to be done for them by the professionals. Intercession before God became the domain of the professional . . . the people came to the organizational priest to confess their sins.

The ministry was now firmly in the hands of the professionals. The New Testament concept of laymen ministering to laymen, with each man functioning as a priest in the marketplace, became a thing of the past.

## Lay Renewal Movements

But godly men saw the distinct difference and distance between the clergy and laity. They didn't like it, for it was in opposition to the teachings of the New Testament. Until the dramatic impact of the Protestant Reformation, these smaller movements had little pervasive influence. But because they show that laity throughout history want to be part of God's program, we will mention a few of these movements or persons:

*The Waldenses.* Peter Waldo . . . twelfth century . . . a merchant from Lyons, France. He wanted to return to the New Testament teachings. The Scriptures were translated into the vernacular, and the laity were encouraged to memorize large portions of them. Convinced that laymen could preach the gospel, the movement spread through France, Italy, Spain, Germany, and Bohemia. The organized church branded them as heretics, and their numbers were scattered and, finally, dissipated.

*John Wyclif.* A native of Yorkshire, England, Wyclif translated the "official" Latin Vulgate Bible into the language of the people and taught that laymen could participate in the ministry—even to the administration of the sacraments. He died a natural death in 1384 but was later condemned by the church. His writings were banned, his bones exhumed and burned, and the ashes were scattered in a stream.

*John Hus.* Influenced by the writings of Wyclif, Hus began preaching to his native Czechs in their language, demanding certain acts of reformation by the church. Condemned, Hus was burned at the stake.

## Protestant Reformation

There were other efforts at reforming the Catholic church, seeking to bring it back to a more biblical posture, but they all fell short of their goal. It wasn't until such "reforming" seeds germinated in a favorable political climate that fruit would be born.

The date was 1517. The place: Wittenberg, Germany. An obscure priest named Martin Luther nailed his grievances to the church door—the Reformation was born. A number of changes were called for by this bold, imaginative priest, but *at the very core of the Reformation was the conviction that all believers were priests of the living God.*

He felt that all believers had the right and responsibility to study God's Word, involve themselves in the ministry, make confession to God on their own, and even administer the sacraments.

## Postreformation Era:
## Development of Lay "Specialty" Groups

Unfortunately, shortly after the Reformation, the vision of the "priesthood of believers" again began to fade in many parts of the Protestant church.

For some, the implications of all believers functioning as priests was never clearly seen and they continued to embrace the Levitical concept. The communion table remained an altar, pastors were called priests, and the distinction between clergy and laity persisted.

Concerned laymen, demanding a hearing, continued to rise to the surface. Nowhere did this picture emerge more clearly than in foreign missions. Again and again laymen were at the vanguard of Protestant efforts to evangelize the world. William Carey, Hudson Taylor, and many like them were *laymen* who went overseas—not sent by the church, but by other concerned laymen who formed "specialty groups" organized to perform specific functions.

In the United States all such mission societies prior to 1820 were lay movements. Some had a close relationship to congregations, but all were funded and administered by laymen. Many, if not most, of the indigenous groups in the United States today were begun as lay missions. Current expressions of these lay movements are Wycliffe Bible Translators, Young Life, Campus Crusade, The Navigators, YMCA, YWCA, Sunday schools, The Evangelical Alliance Mission, Overseas Crusades, Sudan Interior Mission, Youth for Christ, and scores of others. Some of the members of these groups may be theologically trained, but *all are lay movements.*

To view the organized church run by the professionals as the sole legitimate expression of God's ministry is to regress to an Old Testament Levitical perspective. The Reformation represented a partial return to the New Testament pattern of the priesthood of the believer and *although it is preached today, it has yet to find its fullest expression in the body of Christ.* There is still a way to go!

### FOR DISCUSSION

1. Can you, as a layman, function as a "priest" without being professionally trained? If so, why? If not, why not?

2. On page 88 your particular ministry is explained as analogous to a pebble impacting a large pond. How would you define your specific ministry? What part of the pond are you "covering"?

3. In what areas of the Christian life with which you are familiar can you identify the tendency to revert to the Levitical concept of the ministry?

# CHAPTER 8

# HOW MEN AND WOMEN OF GOD ARE PRODUCED

*As a believer grows spiritually, he is influenced by a variety of ministries. All of these ministries, functioning under the orchestration of the Holy Spirit in the maturation of the believer, is the church.*

This chapter will show how men and women of God are produced, how they have developed into who they are—a sort of spiritual "roots" study.

## Produced By a Variety of Ministries

We began this study several years ago by doing a series of case analyses of the lives of "functioning" laymen from around the United States. (We define a functioning disciple as one who knows Christ, feeds himself from the Word, and gives himself away to others. Each person can decide for himself if he is in this category). In our study we discovered that, without exception, these disciples have been *the product of a variety of ministries.* The pattern was repeated time and time again.

Here is a hypothetical illustration of what we discovered (please realize that the organizations mentioned here are *merely examples* of the many of dozens that could have been used):

As a youngster the person may attend Child Evangelism meetings where he first hears the gospel in simply and clear form. During his teens he may come into contact with Young Life, Youth for Christ, or may attend youth meetings in his local congregation. While in college or the military he may meet Campus Crusade, InterVarsity, or The Navigators.

As the individual grows and deepens, he may become involved in a Billy Graham Crusade and may become a counselor. He and his family may attend a Bible Memory Association Camp or may spend a week in the Bill Gothard Basic Youth Conflicts Seminar.

He and his family may participate in a Here's Life project of community evangelism. He then may join the local Christian Businessmen's Committee where he regularly takes his uncommitted associates to the luncheons. All of this time he is part of a local congregation.

This example of multiplicity of ministries and influences that take part in developing the lives of Christians we call a "matrix," which means "that which gives origin or form to a thing." *This matrix that influences each believer is the church.*

A full-rounded disciple needs this type of variety, for *no single group or local congregation can, for his lifetime, fulfill all his growing needs.*

It takes a number of different ministries to enter into a disciple's life at various stages of growth and indelibly make their mark. They help him acquire a grasp on the Word of God, develop a meaningful devotional life, learn how to evangelize, select a proper career, prepare for marriage, move through the various passages into middle age, through the empty-the-nest state, and eventually to grow old gracefully.

A single ministry mentioned above *may* play a predominant role in some Christians' lives, but most disciples are involved with a variety of ministries that forms the matrix of growth. Often more than one group or organization is influencing the growing Christian at any given time. The Holy Spirit brings certain ministries into their lives at special times of need in order to fully equip them for the work of the ministry. All of these ministries functioning under the orchestration of the Holy Spirit in the maturation of the believer is the church.

### An Explanation of the Matrix of Ministries

Illustration #2 gives a simplistic view of the framework for the matrix of ministries. At the

# HOW MEN AND WOMEN OF GOD ARE PRODUCED

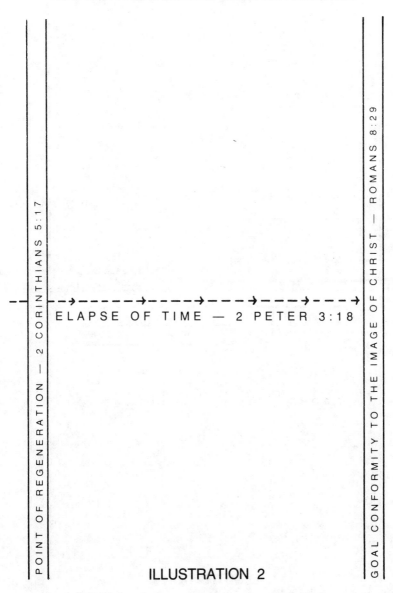

ELAPSE OF TIME — 2 PETER 3:18

POINT OF REGENERATION — 2 CORINTHIANS 5:17

GOAL CONFORMITY TO THE IMAGE OF CHRIST — ROMANS 8:29

**ILLUSTRATION 2**

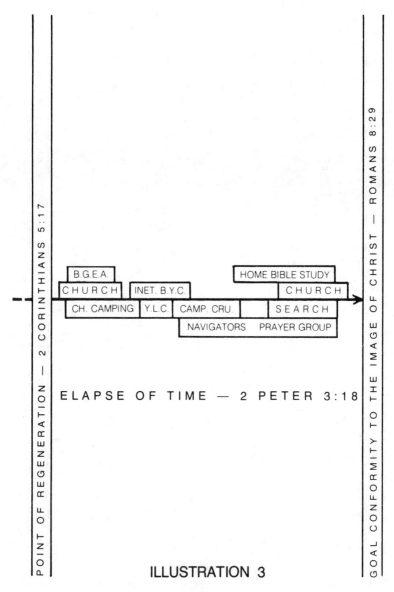

ILLUSTRATION 3

# HOW MEN AND WOMEN OF GOD ARE PRODUCED

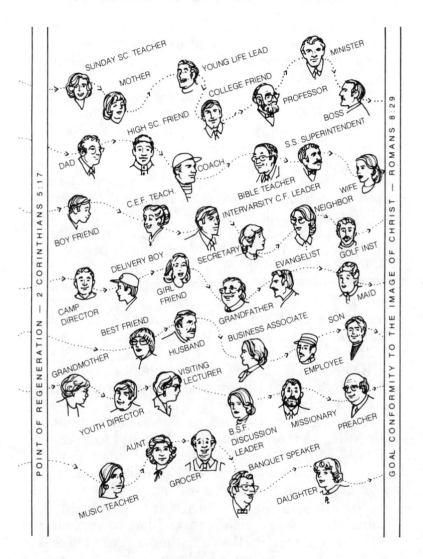

**ILLUSTRATION 4**

point of *regeneration,* the new Christian is freshly born of the Spirit: "Therefore, if anyone is in Christ, he is a new creation; the old has gone, the new has come!" (2 Cor. 5:17).

The *elapse of time* (here measured in years) is when the Holy Spirit is working in a person's life in order to accomplish God's purposes. This is the period of journeying through the matrix of ministries. This is the growing time: "But grow in the grace and knowledge of our Lord and Savior Jesus Christ. To him be glory both now and forever!" (2 Peter 3:18). The amount of time this takes and the various ministries encountered is vastly different from person to person, as the Lord works with each individual uniquely.

The ultimate goal is *conformity to the image of Christ:* "For those God foreknew he also predestined to be conformed to the likeness of his Son, that he might be the firstborn among many brothers" (Rom. 8:29).

Illustration #3 shows an example of the journey of one follower of Christ. The matrix of ministries is as complex as the Holy Spirit wants it to be. And, remember, the use of specifically named ministries in these graphs is only a representation of some of the types of groups involved in developing disciples. Often several ministries overlap as both are helping the person at the same time.

This illustration, to help explain this idea, shows the blocks of influence filled in with the names of *groups,* but the "shepherding of the flock of God among you" is actually done by *individuals* (see Illustration #4).

Illustration #4 shows that the matrix is extremely complex. It consists of people who minister to the disciple. Institutions and organizations don't minister, only people do.

## This Is the Church—The Whole Body of Christ

If the reader concedes that all functioning men and women of God are the product of a multiplicity of influences that have come into their lives via the matrix explanation, and that *one* of those influences is the local congregation (which does not have the total input or influence in the individual's life), then we suggest that *this total process is the church.*

The church cannot be defined as one individual group or influence, but the totality of influences brought to bear by the Holy Spirit in helping a man or woman become a functioning disciple.

If we were to say that the local assembly is the exclusive vehicle of God's program, we would have to admit that, without exception, much of God's maturing process is *every* functioning disciple's life (as shown by the matrix) takes place outside the local congregation. The local assembly plays only a limited role in the growth of the functioning disciple.

It is within this total matrix of influences that the newly regenerated person finds viable, believable models for his own life. The reason is that these models live in a more "real" arena than the vocational clergy do. These lay models, like the new Christian, are learning by experience how to live the Christian life. They are sharing their faith in the daily activities of living: in the neighborhood and in business, all with the attendant pressures, temptations, and stresses.

When the new Christian sees that other lay people can "minister" and can function as "priests," *he learns he can do the same.*

### God's Use of "Specialty Groups"

And this brings the discussion back full circle—to the fact of the historical and biblical development of the priesthood of the believer and God's use of lay "specialty" groups to help continue the process of "every lay person is a priest."

Christ is building His church. And He is on schedule. One of the major ways God has been working in accomplishing His purposes in the building of His church has been in these "specialty" groups.

This is not, in any way, to suggest that the local congregation has been ignored or is unnecessary in the task of world evangelism. Rather, it is to draw attention to the potent force these specialty groups have been in the program of God. They have given fledgling believers a clear sense of mission.

Their call, by and large, is task-oriented—a call to individuals to reach their sphere of influence for Christ. These groups make up much of the matrix of ministries.

C.I. Scofield said, "The commission to evangelize the world is personal and not corporate." These specialty groups have made the mission of the church personal, as distinguished from corporate or institutional. It is to this mission that laity have been eagerly responding, resulting in the phenomenal growth the church is currently experiencing.

An ecclesiastical mobilization of laymen to fulfill an inadequate mission of the church is doomed to failure. God's program has always been people—never organizations. This is seen scripturally and empirically in the way the Holy Spirit raises up men and women of God!

**FOR DISCUSSION**

1. In considering the "matrix of ministries" and the organizations that have most contributed to your life:

What are the key organizations that helped you develop?

What areas of growth did each one contribute to?

What organization is now most influential in your life?

How is the current organization ministering to you?

2. What is your local congregation contributing to your life now?

3. What areas of ministry skills do you feel you are lacking? How are you getting help in these areas? Where can you get help?

4. As a lay person, do you intensely desire to have a "slice of the action" for God in the marketplace? Are you doing it? If not, why not?

5. Who are the individuals who have had the most significant spiritual impact on your life? With what organizations or institutions were they associated?

# CHAPTER 9

# THE ROLE OF THE LOCAL CONGREGATION IN THE LAYMAN'S GROWTH

*No believer is the exclusive possession of any single group, whether it be the local assembly or a "specialty" group.*

How does the local assembly fit into this "matrix of ministries"? Obviously, it should play a sustained and critical role.

This role can be explained simply by the analogy of the relationship of parents to the family. As a variety of influences shape the life of the growing child (school, clubs, scouts, camping programs, athletics, friends, etc.), the parents are the ones who provide continuity, stability, balance, and perspective. The role of the parents is to equip the child for a life of productive service.

The key role of the local congregation is to equip the disciple for a life of productive service for God. The local assembly provides continuity and stability.

But there are two areas of potential conflict in relating to the church: one is the fault of the pastor and the other is the fault of the member.

## ✗ Conflict Caused by the Pastor

The first conflict is evident when congregations view the complexity of the matrix and become disturbed or threatened. Laymen report that the "matrix of ministries" seems to threaten many pastors. And when pastors claim that they, and they alone, are exclusively in control of the spiritual development of each individual in their fold, they are becoming overly possessive of their members.

Returning to the analogy of the family, difficulties occur when parents become too possessive and refuse to allow the child to mature into a healthy independence. This attitude will also create difficulties within the local assembly. For example, a minister cannot say that he does not want anyone else telling *his* members how to live a Christ-centered life!

There is the persistent claim that whatever is done in the ministry of the gospel of Jesus Christ "ought" to be done through and under the authority of the local congregation. Such viewpoints stem from an inadequate understanding of the church as presented in the Scriptures and from an incomplete acceptance of the "priesthood of the believer."

Let it be noted here that *no believer is the exclusive possession of any single group,* whether the local assembly or "specialty" group. As a parent, God has entrusted to my care children to be nurtured and trained to be His faithful servants. They are not "my children—they belong to Him. Failure to recognize this is invariably counterproductive to my God-given task as a parent.

Also, in the assembly, a possessive, competitive spirit is counterproductive to the work of God. The pastor is to "feed" the sheep, but Jesus called them "My sheep." They belong to the Shepherd of their souls.

All Christians should rejoice at the progress seen in people's lives as they move closer to God and become productive in His kingdom—irrespective of the ministry that is currently influencing them. This type of creativity of the Holy Spirit is a lesson for all believers.

## Conflict Caused by the Layman

The second area of potential conflict is seen in the immature response some laymen have toward their local congregation. Frequently, when a person is influenced by the broad "matrix of ministries," he asks, "Why didn't my pastor give me this?" He becomes suspicious or resentful of the local assembly and its leadership because it has not met his expectations. He perceives his communion as having drifted away from a biblical base or having programs to which he is opposed. This type of disgruntled layman should read the second chapter of this book and embrace the scriptural content there.

Because of his resentment, the dissatisfied layman becomes determined to change the course and direction of the local congregation. This is understandable because he has a long-term commitment with that group. But when this determination, born out of frustration, becomes the overriding concern or a crusade of his life, it becomes a luxury of the flesh he simply cannot afford. The cost in terms of resources and emotional energy drain is too high. The mature man of God won't stay in a frustrating situation, waiting until he can "reform" the local congregation. He should adopt a more positive posture, thus utilizing his energies for the promotion of the gospel.

In summary, local congregations must not feel possessive or threatened when the "matrix of ministries" influences its members. As important as the local assembly is, it is only *part* of God's program of raising up men after His own heart. And people who have grown within the matrix should not look askance at the local congregation and develop unrealistic expectations of it. (See the last chapter of this book for recommendations for both pastors and local congregation members on how they can cooperate more effectively).

Balance must be maintained as the disciple relates to His program: "There is one body and one Spirit—just as you were called to one hope when you were called—" (Eph. 4:4).

**FOR DISCUSSION**

1. What role does your local assembly play in your life?

2. What role are you playing in your local assembly?

3. If you are a "sheep" as described in the first chapter, is someone helping you become a disciple?

4. Do you feel your local congregation will allow you to freely develop a ministry in your vocation in the marketplace? If not, why not?

# CHAPTER 10

# THE LAYMAN AND INSTITUTIONALISM

*If a person knew he had but one week to live, he wouldn't invest the time in building an addition to his home. When the church lives in the expectancy of the imminent return of Christ, it does not invest its time and resources in the construction of the institution.*

One of the reasons we spend a chapter discussing institutions is because laymen are intricately involved with them, whether in the church or in religious "specialty" groups. Laymen get frustrated with encrusted institutionalism, for they are eager to be an active and viable part of God's program.

Institutionalism is legitimate . . . to a point. But when carried too far, it has a calcifying nature. Then the aims and workings of institutions are often at odds with what is best for the individual.

Though the Lord is in the business of redeeming and working through people, not institutions, there are legitimate reasons for developing and establishing institutions.

## Reasons for Institutions

*Man is a societal being.* This is how God created him. The recluse is rare. Most people need the various supports the community offers. To develop institutions or organizations to facilitate this societal tendency in man is natural and normal.

*Common goals and objectives.* Whenever a group of people agree on a common direction, the natural thing to do is to organize. This assists in reaching the objective. It may be as simple as a group of homeowners organizing to agree on covenants to maintain their property value . . . or others on how to worship God in a certain way.

*Economy of force.* Mickey Marcus, a U.S. Army Colonel, went to Israel in 1948 to help the various guerrilla factions unite into an effective army. In order to demonstrate to the Israeli commanders the "economy of force" principle, Marcus thumped his left hand with each of his fingers on his right hand. These individual thumps combined did not equal the power of the five fingers clenched into a fist. The corporate effort of people functioning in concert is more effective than isolated individual efforts.

*Spiritual gifts.* From a Christian perspective, Paul gives still another reason for organizing. First Corinthians 12–14 teaches that the Holy Spirit has distributed His gifts in such a way that no one has them all. Having them all would make an individual totally independent. Instead, everyone has at least one, thus making him an important part of the whole. Even in secular society, the combining of gifts and talents provides a reason for people to form institutions.

However, difficulties arise in Christendom when the "matrix of ministries" is not fully understood and when the local congregation attempts to have laymen conform to an institutional image of "what a good Christian should be." This is because the church has become encrusted with institutionalism.

## How Institutionalism Harms the Church

1. *Competition.* Malcolm Muggeridge says, "Christianity is not a statistical religion." Christians need constant reminders that this is so. Moses said of Israel, "The LORD did not set his affection on you and choose you because you were more numerous than other peoples, for you were the fewest of all peoples" (Deut. 7:7).

William Diehl in *Christianity and Real Life* said,

101

". . . my church sees lay ministry purely in terms of service to the institutional church. My church proclaims the ministry of lay persons *in the world,* it practices the encouragement of lay ministries solely *within the church* . . ." (emphasis ours).

Much thinking and strategizing is programmed toward institutional goals, for that means larger membership. Each leader, it seems, wants the best, the most, the biggest!

2. *Loss of the sense of the imminent return of Christ.* An article in the *Encyclopedia Brittanica* explains the dying out of first-century expectations of an imminent return of Jesus and its replacement by a spirit of institutional self-preservation against the world.

The spirit of philosophical and theological speculation and of ethical reflection, which began to spread through the Churches, did not know what to make of the old hopes of the future. To a new generation they seemed paltry, earthly and fantastic, and far-seeing men had good reason to regard them as a source of political danger.

But more than this, these wild dreams about the glorious kingdom of Christ began to disturb the organization which the Churches had seen fit to introduce. In the interests of self-preservation against the world, the State and the heretics, the Christian communities had formed themselves into compact societies with a definite creed and constitution, and they felt that their existence was threatened by the white heat of religious subjectivity.

Rather than an organism that ministered to a lost world by a pervasive impact on the lives of individuals in that world, it transitioned into an organization with creeds, government and well-defined institutional goals that involved it politically and diplomatically in the affairs of nations and the whole world.

If a person knew he had a week to live, he wouldn't invest it in building an addition to his home. If the church lives in the expectancy of the imminent return of Christ, it does not invest its time and resources in the construction of the institution. Yet the whole variety of ministry "matrix" that comprises today's evangelical church believes in the imminent return of Christ more so than in any century since the first!

3. *"Getting off the hook."* Some people join organizations because it takes them "off the hook" spiritually. The tendency is to allow the organization to define what involvement in the ministry means. The organization is happy to do this for the person because it means one more faithful member. The person likewise is eager, for it means he does not have to get before God and determine the part God would have him play in the work of the ministry. The organization will do this for him, and it is all too tempting to join one that makes minimal demands.

4. *Management by objectives.* The natural tendency, particularly among laymen, is to incorporate the practices and principles applied to busi-

ness into the Christian sphere. This is nowhere more evident than in the use of the principles of the American Management Association and particularly, the concept of Management by Objectives (MBO). But when MBO is applied to the church, it creates tremendous difficulties.

In the New Testament the analogy used for the ministry is the family, *not business*. The illustrations have to do with the shepherd caring for the sheep, the father-son relationship, the nurse with her children. Growth, maturing, and adulthood . . . these are words used to describe the discipling process. But because a layman has success in the business arena, the natural tendency is to incorporate the same principles into his ministry, not realizing that the ministry is not analogous to business. It should be more analogous to the family.

A frequently used definition of management is "accomplishing work through others." This is illustrative of the fact that in business one uses or "buys" people to accomplish predetermined goals and objectives. When a man works for a corporation, he is allowing that corporation to *use* him for certain financial remuneration. The corporation will then motivate him by any means it can to get him to produce the maximum amount in accordance with its goals and objectives.

In the Christian ministry the goal is not to use or manipulate people to accomplish company goals, but to minister to people to help them become effective servants of Jesus Christ. The goal of organization should be to help the individual accomplish his objectives, not vice versa. Goals and objectives, therefore, must be a very personal matter and cannot be conditioned on the performance of other people. Once a person makes his goal conditional on the performance of others, he has a difficult time resisting the temptation of manipulating those people toward helping him accomplish his goals.

The work of God can neither be measured nor controlled. MBO is a subtle endeavor to do both. It simply cannot be done in the ministry. When tried it builds frustration and resentment in the lives of people who are part of its process . . . and they may not even be able to articulate exactly why they feel frustrated.

5. *Measure and control.* Man is never quite so uncomfortable as when he cannot control and measure his activities. The New Testament concept of the church is seen as an organism rather than an institution. But because an organism defies control and measurement, man intuitively surrenders his freedom and institutionalizes the church. His desire to control and measure is satisfied, his insecurities are abated, and the grace of God is prostituted.

The process of the "matrix of ministries" is orchestrated by the Holy Spirit, not by man. He brings others into the disciple's life in order to conduct His ministry to him.

There is no way to measure the impact of one's ministry. The business world does measure what it does: i.e. the production of automobiles, the P & L statement, etc. But the essential ingredient in the walk of a disciple is that he walks by faith. If he could measure and control, he wouldn't have to walk by *faith*. He would know, because he would see it all measured out on paper and in graphs.

The inability to measure or control the work of God does not eliminate goal setting or accountability. Each person is accountable not only to God, but also to others for proper behavior . . . but not for how many disciples or converts he "produces."

Each individual is responsible to determine before God what His will is. Most of what He does is qualitative. Because this cannot be measured the tendency is to shift evaluation to quantitative measurements. Such an evaluation may tangentially touch the work of God, but to draw a circle around it and say that this is what God is doing is fallacious.

## The "Dead" Church

At every meeting dealing with the layman and his ministry, there is the inevitable question, "Where do I fit in a 'dead' church?"

Some of the factors of institutionalism, as given above, help create a dead church. Generally, a layman feels his church is dead if his spiritual needs are not being met.

In the case of denominations there are often strong family ties and there is no alternative attractive enough to encourage changing. What to do?

*First,* realize this isn't an isolated problem. William Diehl, in *Christianity and Real Life,* identifies the same problem in his own denominational relationship, revealing that it is more typical than churchmen in general would like to admit:

> When my church preaches about the ministry of the laity, it speaks in broad and idealistic terms, but when it comes down to reality, my church sees lay ministry purely in terms of service to the institutional church. My church proclaims the ministry of lay persons in the world; it practices the encouragement of lay ministries solely within the church—in teaching, leading worship, visiting members, serving on local, regional, and national committees, and giving time and money to the organization. I believe this gap is not intentional. Furthermore, I believe it can be bridged.

Diehl is even optimistic as he states the problem, feeling that the gap can be bridged. It is with this expectation that the reader progresses through his book, but later Diehl begins to waver:

> . . . most lay members of our churches today maintain that the church is not helping them to relate their faith to their life.

Then near the end of the book, Diehl feels it probably *can't* bridge the gap, as he earlier indicated could be done, for he says:

> It is unfortunate that many who are already engaged in vital lay ministries are among those who say they are unable to connect their Sunday world to their weekday world. The fault, of course, lies in the fact that the religious institution is incapa-

ble of recognizing and affirming lay ministries beyond its own walls.

Numerous other testimonies are available to demonstrate this level of frustration for one reason or another, and any person feeling this way tends to think his own situation is unique. With "super churches" described to him in magazines, church growth books, and by visiting ministers, the layman tends to become discouraged by a feeling of growing hopelessness.

*Second,* make sure that the local congregation is evaluated in terms of the "sheep and disciples" concept as explained in the second chapter of this book.

*Third,* realize that no church will be perfect. There is no basic New Testament church in history that was fully healthy and pure and that can furnish us with a model we can emulate.

In Matthew 13:24–30 Jesus warns us that the church will be a mixture of "wheat and tares"—good and bad. It has always been so and will remain so until He comes again. To expect a perfect fellowship is to expect something Jesus promised we could not have this side of heaven. It has been said, "If you ever find the perfect assembly, don't join it. If you do, it will cease being perfect."

We are nothing more than a group of sinners in whose life the Holy Spirit is patiently working to remake us into the image of Jesus Christ.

The Holy Spirit is transforming individuals, not institutions. Let us not spend our time and energy on institutions when God has invited us to co-labor with Him in investing in the lives of people. Improvement in institutions can come only through inprovement in individuals who comprise the institution.

Jesus will have most of us work in the context of "the church as a formal and established institution," but the building of the institution is not the work of God. God may use it in His work; but His work is not the saving, sanctifying, or building of institutions: it is *people.*

## The Positive Example of the Billy Graham Association

Too often a denomination sees itself as being the entire function of the body of Christ in a given locality—out of necessity. It feels it and it alone is in charge of evangelism, that all youth work must be done under its auspices and preferably on its premises, and that financial support of missionary enterprises can properly be done only by funneling the assets through its missionary committee.

Contrast this viewpoint with that of the Billy Graham Evangelistic Association which sees itself purely as a ministry of *evangelism*—and nothing else!

A minister once commented on this, indicating that Mr. Graham had missed a higher contribution to Christendom because of keeping his ministry too narrow. The minister lamented the fact that Mr. Graham had not attended seminary, thus depth and substance was missing from his preaching. The man said that Mr. Graham was "still preaching the same old simple stuff."

Hundreds of people have dreamed up new emphases and directions for Mr. Graham to follow throughout all these years, but thankfully he has resisted the allurements of "bigger and better" opportunities and has restricted his vision to the very narrow ministry to which God called him.

This form of criticism of Billy Graham is typified by this comment from *The Young Evangelicals*, by Richard Quebedeaux:

> If mainstream Ecumenical Liberals in the past criticized Billy Graham for his appeal to the emotions (something few Liberals would do today), they now feel that he is wrong in neglecting a unique opportunity to influence the highest circles of political life for the cause of social righteousness. Liberals and some Evangelicals are increasingly disturbed by Graham's present disregard for the social dimension of the Gospel . . .

Notice the difference in emphasis as maintained by Mr. Graham vs. those who have a "more perfect way" for his life. Whereas he is content to specialize in the narrow confines of the ministry to which God has called him, his critics have grandiose schemes for him to be "more things to more men."

Mr. Graham has been content to be himself and to recognize the specific call that God has given him. He is content to merely encourage those other activities, places of service and specialties which, together with his ministry, comprise the body of Christ operating during his generation.

There is a paradox here. By Mr. Graham's strict adherence to his specialized call, he probably has the largest overview of and contact with the body of Christ of anyone in this generation. This is attributable in no small part to his willingness not to compete with anyone else, but to be an intelligent, concerned encouragement to all the other missions that are laboring alongside him in the body of Christ. This is surely the unity of which Christ prayed in John 17:21, "that all of them may be one, Father, just as you are in me and I am in you. May they also be in us so that the world may believe that you have sent me."

For the sake of illustration, the total work of God in an individual's life can be likened to a pie. The ministering disciple has two choices as he helps another: 1) he can say that the whole pie is his responsibility (i.e., that he is responsible for all that God is doing in the other's life). Or 2) he can say that only one slice of the pie is his responsibility (i.e., that he is responsible for only part of what God is doing in the other's life).

To the degree that the disciple elects option 1, he becomes insular, myopic, competitive, and self-sufficient. He has no need for the rest of the body of Christ.

To the degree that he elects option 2, he becomes dependent on the rest of the body to help contribute to the lives of those to whom he is ministering. He then becomes more appreciative of others as well as dependent on them for the work that God wants to accomplish through his life.

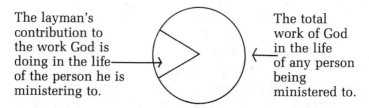

The layman's contribution to the work God is doing in the life of the person he is ministering to.

The total work of God in the life of any person being ministered to.

Billy Graham has defined his slice of the pie very narrowly (evangelism) and trusts God to bring whatever matrix of ministries necessary into the lives of the people to help them in their spiritual quest. This is, in part, the reason for his entree to the rest of the body. They do not feel in competition with him.

A man must be able to see what God has called him to do and be able to say no to those pressures that detract him from his calling, while at the same time appreciating what God has called others to do. Generally speaking, the narrower the slice of one's pie, the greater one's appreciation for the rest of the body of Christ.

## The Place of Organizations

Lewis Sperry Chafer in his *Systematic Theology*, Volume 5, speaking of ecclesiastical organizations, says:

> Organization is wisdom's first step for a people associated together in a common cause; but organization is for a purpose and therefore is not the purpose itself. Sectarianism tends to a neglect of the purpose—that which actuates every worthy church—and to magnify the organization.

Howard Snyder in *The Problem of Wine Skins* says, "Christians must see themselves as the community of God's people, not in the first place as members of organizations."

This same idea was articulated twenty-five years ago by J. B. Phillips in *Your God Is Too Small:*

> The thoughtful man outside the Churches is not offended so much by the *differences* of denominations. To him, in his happy ignorance, these are merely the normal psychological variations of human taste and temperament being expressed in the religious sphere. What he cannot stomach is the exclusive claim made by each to be the "right one."
>
> His judgment is rightly empirical—did not Christ say, "By their fruits ye shall know them"? If he were to observe that the church which makes the boldest and most exclusive claim to be constituted and maintained according to Almighty God's own ideas was obviously producing the finest Christian character, obviously wielding the highest Christian influence, and obviously most filled by the living Spirit of God—he could perhaps forgive the exclusive claim. *But he finds nothing of the kind.*
>
> No denomination has a monopoly of God's grace and none has an exclusive recipe for producing Christian character. It is quite plain to the disinterested observer that the real God takes no notice whatever of boxes: "the Spirit bloweth where it listeth" and is subject to no regulation of man.

Organizations are valid tools in drawing people together for a common cause. Too easily, however, these organizations become ends in themselves. They move from being self seeking to being insular and sectarian.

This tendency not only plagues already established institutions, but frequently cuts short the life of the specialty groups. The purpose and distinction for which they came into existence fades and the organization evolves into the posture of becoming an end in itself.

There is a direct correlation between viewing the organization as an end in itself and viewing the task of world evangelism institutionally. Specialty groups have been able to marshal the laity because they say, "The ministry is your responsibility. God has called you to penetrate your arena with the Gospel."

When any group embraces the mentality that says the organization is supreme and that God has given the task of discipling the nations to their organization, their ability to enlist laymen to their cause weakens considerably.

## Dedication to That Which Is Eternal

Because all people are emotionally involved in the success of more than one organization or institution, it is difficult to remain objective when those beloved institutions are critically scrutinized. In the course of this book we are not attempting to depreciate organizations; but, rather, to view them from the perspective of what God is doing in history.

*People are eternal; institutions are temporal.* Whatever the institution, it is like a building or piece of furniture: someday it will cease to be. Dick Halverson, in an interview in *The Wittenburg Door,* said:

> What's happening now is a dissolution of religious institutions as we know them. They're cracking and crumbling a lot more than anybody can see from the outside or inside.
>
> Jesus said that when you put new wine into old wineskins, two things happen. One, the new wine is spilled. I think the new wine of the Spirit that's been poured out by God over the last quarter century has not been contained by the institutional church and it's spilling out. A lot more is happening for Christ in the world outside of the institutional church than inside.
>
> The second thing that happens is the old wineskins are destroyed. They simply cannot stretch to accommodate the new things that are happening so they begin cracking and finally collapse.

The church as an institution is temporal. Only when one refers to the church as the people of God is it eternal. The church's organizational expressions will go the way of all institutions.

One's goal should never be the preservation of the organization but the worth of the individual. Whenever the institution sacrifices the individual for its own goals, while justifying its action on the grounds of the "common good," it is embracing a value system different than that which is God's.

### FOR DISCUSSION

1. Are any of the five factors on pages 101–106 evident in your local congregation?

2. Which ones are? Explain how each is manifested?

3. What do you think can be done about these?

4. Are you anticipating Christ's return? How is this evident in your daily existence?

5. Have you joined to "get off the hook"? Explain.

6. Have you joined because you "need to belong"? Explain.

7. Do you personally feel that you can totally "train or disciple" another person, without help from others in the body of Christ. If so, why? If not, why not?

8. Are you giving yourself to that which is eternal?

9. What are some positive benefits you have accrued in belonging to institutions?

10. Are there any institutions of which you are a part that tend to use people in the accomplishment of organizational goals rather than help them? What practical ways can you remain part of this institution while resisting this tendency?

# CHAPTER 11

# CHRIST IS BUILDING HIS CHURCH

*Jesus said, ". . . I will build my church, and the gates of Hades will not overcome it."*

Before the laity can be mobilized into action as stressed in Part I of this book, it is essential to understand the mission of the church . . . for the ministry is, after all, the work of the total body of Christ.

## Confusion About the Mission of the Church

Ambiguous statements are being written about the mission of the Church:

117

1. *The mission is to penetrate the community for Christ.* John R. W. Stott, the British theologian-pastor, holds this view. In his book *Christian Mission in the Modern World,* he says, "When any community deteriorates, the blame should be attached where it belongs; not to the community which is going bad but to the church which is failing in its responsibility as salt to stop it going bad" (page 32). He is saying that if a city is in need of biblical solutions, the responsibility rests with the corporate church rather than with individual believers.

2. *The church does not have the responsibility for the community.* C.I. Scofield says, "Much is said concerning the 'mission of the church.' The 'church which is his body' has for its mission to build itself up until the body is complete, but the visible church, as such, is charged with no mission. The commission to evangelize the world is personal and not corporate."

3. *World-wide evangelism is the task of the church.* The Lausanne Congress on World Evangelization concluded, ". . . In the church's mission of sacrificial service, evangelism is primary. World evangelisation requires the whole church to take the whole gospel to the whole world. The church is at the very center of God's cosmic purpose and is his appointed means of spreading the gospel. . . ."

This agrees with Stott, in part, but goes even further in suggesting that world-wide evangelism is the task of the institutional church. It is interesting to note that the Billy Graham Evangelistic Association, which sponsored the Lausanne Conference, is not even included in the charge to evangelize—that responsibility, according to Lausanne's Article 6, belongs to the church.

4. *The mission is to create an environment of fellowship, affirmation, and encouragement.* The late Dr. D. Martyn Lloyd-Jones, who was one of Britain's great evangelical churchmen, said, "Today priority must be given anew to the doctrine of the church. Too many people regard institutional organizations as the church. I believe in *evangelical ecumenism.* I believe evangelicals should combine forces—not to form a new denomination, but for fellowship and cooperation. Such mutual strenghtening is the hopeful way into the future."

These different viewpoints are simply illustrative of the ambiguity in Christ's body regarding the church's mission. Though threads of similarity can be taken from these definitions, all with some validity, their inconsistency with one another points to the chilling fact that nineteen hundred years after Christ's declaration of purpose the church still has difficulty in defining its mission.

This cacaphony of voices disagreeing on the nature and mission of the church, even within evangelicalism, creates uncertainty among the laity. The trumpet is giving an uncertain sound. If the leadership of the organized church cannot agree where it is going and thus fails to articulate its mission to laymen, *how can it challenge and involve its people?*

## Christ Is Building His Church

The confusion regarding the mission of the church in no way hinders *His* building of His church. There is a strong, clear voice on Jesus' building of the church. It is stated by Christ Himself in Matthew 16:18, "'And I tell you that you are Peter, and on this rock I will build my church, and the gates of Hades will not overcome it.'"

Historically, Christendom has viewed these words as foundational to the church. Notice that it is a declaration and not an appeal. It is not conditioned on what the disciples or those who follow them will do. Rather it is a statement of what *He* will do. No response is asked and no spirit of cooperation is solicited. "I will build *my* church." From start to finish, it is the program of the sovereign Creator of the universe.

And, since He is sovereign, it is safe to assume that His program of building the church is right on schedule. Not a day late . . . not an hour early. Furthermore, He is not bound to use the institutional church apparatus we have created and which has become so dear to us.

Martin Luther, the father of the Protestant Reformation, also wrestled with the concept of the church. Heinrich Bornkamm, in his book *Luther's World of Thought,* discusses this in detail in a chapter entitled "What is the Church?" Bornkamm gives Luther's understanding of what the church is:

The believers, who hear and preserve the Word of God, are the church.

The dividing power of the Word eliminates the multitude of nominal Christians from the true believers, i.e. the church. The church is not a visible organization; it extends all over the world.

This is one great truth proclaimed by Luther on the church: The church is the people of God living from the Word of God. This communion of believers in Christ is the one holy Christian Church on earth. Again and again the question has been raised: Is this not saying too little? What about local congregations and state churches? Are they not also church? Here Luther differentiated very logically.

He always chafed a bit under the term "church"; in the first place, because, as the name for a building made of stone, it is misleading and ill suited to the communion of believers ... secondly, because it had become customary to apply the term "church" also to the properly constituted congregations. Luther follows this custom only reluctantly, since many congregations bear little resemblance to the body of Christ.

He expresses surprise that St. Paul uses the word "church" when speaking of the congregations in Galatia, which grieved him so much. He explains this by saying that Paul does so because of the fraction of church hidden in them, because of those divine gifts, Word and Sacrament, and the life inevitably flowing from them.

Therefore these congregations are called churches with the same validity with which a coin may be termed a gold piece even though it is not 100 percent gold. They contain church as an ore may contain gold. Thus there is always a dividing line running through the congregations—rather through the hearts of those who want to be Christians. With one part of their heart they belong to the church, but with another part they still belong to the world. It cannot be otherwise, since Christ is always the center of controversy, even in the heart of a Christian. Therefore, the church is never a triumphant and perfect quantity; it is always a hidden and struggling power, a power that is often regarded as extinct, but suddenly comes to life again.

But this did not go far enough for people who were anxiously concerned about the reality of the church. They thought it was a disparagement of the church.

The church is also an outward sociological institution as, e.g., the state, cities, guilds, etc., are. At first this second concept occupies a very secondary position, but gradually it is thrust forward, and finally a second, equally justifiable concept of church was adopted . . . the visible church at the side of the invisible. This division into two parts is never found in Luther. It stands to reason that the visible church is of far greater interest to theologians, church politicians, and particularly to the jurists.

Finally, the Lutherans followed in the train of Calvin: The invisible church is disposed of with the elaboration of a few principles, and with a reverential bow it is ushered into heaven. Then exclusive attention is directed to the tangible problems of the so-called visible church. In this way a new legal form of the church developed. It is an institution of public life and may be defined as

such according to form, purpose, personal relationships, etc., as other sociological entities are.
Thereby Luther's profound and unified concept of
the church was destroyed. (© 1958 Concordia
Publishing House. Used by permission.)

Howard Snyder, in his provocative book, *The
Problem of Wine Skins,* discusses the church as it
is presented in the New Testament. He says:

We see that biblically the church is the people of
God and the fellowship of the Holy Spirit, not an
organizational institution. But when we look at
the contemporary church, we see not only (or even
primarily) the church as people; we find also a
proliferation of denominations, institutions, agencies, associations and buildings to which the
name *church* is applied. The Bible does not speak
of such institutions and structures.

Snyder says that Christ's Body is not character-
ized by a particular culture, language, liturgy,
form, or system of government . . . not that these
are wrong, for they are inevitable when believers
gather together and organize. The New Testament
church, however, transcends these.

The simplest definition of the church is Matthew 18:20, ". . . where two or three come together
in my name. . . ." In the New Testament there are
114 references to "church." Of these 85 refer to the
*believers* in a given geographical locale. *Without
exception,* a local church included *all* the believers in that particular community . . . not any single
organizational expression of the church.

If, for example, Paul were to write a letter to the

city of Chicago today, the church there would include *all* Christian elements in that city, everything from local congregations to all of the "specialty" groups and anything in between.

The church is not a building; it is people . . . and, interestingly enough, the bulk of these people are *lay men and lay women.*

## God's Program Has Been People

It is tantalizing to reflect on how God would write history. How would it be different than that written by historians? In one sense this is known, because He did write the history of the Old Testament and the first few years of the New Testament church.

God, in His infinite wisdom, chose Israel as the object of His affection to demonstrate to the nations of the world His character and greatness. Israel is a model of how God deals with His own. In Israel's history can be seen God's faithfulness in pursuing a rebellious people, His chastisement of them when they err, and His unconditional acceptance of them irrespective of their performance. The nations are invited to look on God's dealings with Israel and be instructed (Isa. 51:4–5).

The Lord established institutions in Israel such as the Levitical priesthood and even blessed man-made institutions such as the monarchy. *But the institution is never central; the people of God always are.* His people are His chosen inheritance (Deut. 32:9), and even during times of apostacy He is faithfully calling them to Himself.

124

When man views history he sees institutions; when God views history He sees people. Man's propensity to view institutions as being the ultimate good can easily cloud his ability to perceive what God is doing.

Secular historians did not consider the conversion of Nebuchadnezzer sufficiently important to record it, but God did (Dan. 4:28–37). Conversely, Babylon was raised up as a scourge to discipline Israel. God's prophets carefully explained this nation's role in Israel's destiny, but Babylon, in her strength and power, began to view herself as an end rather than a means to an end. In her self-importance she ignored the role God had given her in history (Jer. 50–51).

Nations never have impressed God. Isaiah views them as "a drop in a bucket" and like "dust on the scales" (Isa. 40:15). The rise and fall of institutions —whether they be nations or corporate bodies within nations—has never been of particular concern to the Lord. His program is bigger than institutions; it is wrapped up in His people. He may bless and use institutions, but He does not expend emotional energy over them and He certainly views them as expendable. Not so with His people. He has voluntarily bound up His own final happiness with the happiness of His people!

Men write history in terms of the rise and demise of institutions. People are "great" to the degree that they relate to these institutions: some because they created them (e.g., Caesar); and some because they destroyed them (e.g., Hitler).

Hebrews 11 introduces us to God's "key men

and women," only a few of whom were even related to institutions . . . and none of the institutions to which they were related are listed as being significant. These people are listed and are important because they came to grips with the greatness of God.

For illustration, look at two of those listed who were related to institutions. The first is Joseph, Hebrews 11:22. Most of the last fourteen chapters of Genesis are devoted to him. Rejected by his brothers and sold into captivity, he rises in the monarchy of Egypt second in rank only to Pharaoh. In his position, he provided for the seven years of famine and, in the process, saved his family.

But note why God considers Joseph great: "By faith Joseph, when his end was near, spoke about the exodus of the Israelites from Egypt and gave instructions about his bones" (Heb. 11:22).

He isn't mentioned because of his position of prominence in Egypt's heirarchy (he is next in line to the Pharaoh), but because he asked some friends to dig up his bones and take them to Canaan when his father's household returned to their homeland!

Why is this important? Because it showed that Joseph was primarily concerned with being part of God's program in history. Being prime minister in Egypt was an exercise in insignificance to Joseph. This high position could easily have turned the head of a man less devoted to God, but Joseph didn't live by the world's system. He had a higher value system: being involved in what God was doing! Taking his bones back to Canaan was a testimonial to the children of Israel that his value system was still intact. Because he held a high position in Egypt, he could have been buried in pomp and luxury in a pyramid. He chose not to do that—for he lived and breathed thoughts of God . . . not his worldly power!

Moses is the second illustration. He led the newly created institution of Israel for eighty years. In a sense, he was the "George Washington" of Israel. Hebrews 11:24-28 records his eulogy in the Hall of Fame:

> By faith Moses, when he had grown up, refused to be known as the son of Pharaoh's daughter. He chose to be mistreated along with the people of God rather than to enjoy the pleasures of sin for a short time. He regarded disgrace for the sake of Christ as of greater value than the treasures of Egypt, because he was looking ahead to his reward. By faith he left Egypt, not fearing the king's anger; he persevered because he saw him who is invisible. By faith he kept the Passover and the sprinkling of blood, so that the destroyer of the firstborn would not touch the firstborn of Israel.

No mention is made of his creating or leading an institution. He is great because he chose to suffer with the people of God rather than enjoy the pleasures of sin.

The comments in this book on the inherent dangers of institutionalism may sound harsh at times, but we suggest that it is also realistic. The authors are not suggesting that organizations be eliminated. An organization in and of itself is not evil, but it does tend to gravitate toward excess.

Create organizations where they are necessary. Often they can serve a useful function in providing its constituents with the tools and vehicles for ministry. Use them and recognize their legitimacy in moving toward the accomplishment of the task. But, above all, do not make them an end in themselves.

Nowhere in the Bible is the Christian called upon to lay down his life for or give his life in exchange for an institution. Jesus said, "Greater love has no one than this, that one lay down his life for his friends" (John 15:13). We are called upon to sacrifice ourselves for *people*. Christ did just that for us.

## Conclusion

After nineteen centuries the ecclesiastical structure is still struggling to identify its mission. Paralleling this is the fact that the Holy Spirit not only has a clear picture of His mission, but He is right on schedule. Through the centuries He has consistently singled out individuals to lead and accomplish His purposes. God is in control and His schedule is up to the minute; His purposes haven't been thwarted.

The responsibility for the ministry does not belong to the institutional church nor does it belong primarily to the clergy. *The responsibility for the ministry belongs first and foremost to the ordinary layman functioning for Christ in the sphere of his own influence.*

The great commission was given to individuals, not to the institutional church. This is the reason why nowhere in the epistles is the great commission reemphasized. In many of the epistles and especially in the first three chapters of Revelation, the institutional church is taken to task for a variety of ills, but nowhere in their myriad of problems are they reprimanded for their lack of evangelistic outreach. The reason for this is that it is not the reponsibility of the institutional church to reach out. The responsibility of the church is the up-building of itself to the glory of God.

Church growth, in the numerical sense, does not come through corporate evangelistic enterprises. Church growth comes through the individual members reaching out into their world, winning and reproducing themselves in the lives of their uncommitted friends. The professional's job is to serve, to equip, and to assist the ordinary layman in this task. He is to "make disciples" as is inherent in the Great Commission (Matt. 28: 18–20). The content of all the epistles deals with the maturation process of the body of Christ. These New Testament letters do not deal with the quantitative growth of the church through evangelism, but with the qualitative inner growth of the church.

The organization can be useful in the program of God, but it becomes counterproductive when people become enamored by it. Individuals, not organizations, are central in Christ's program of building HIS church.

Laymen can play a strategic role in helping redeem a lost and broken humanity. "I looked for a *man* among them who would build up the wall and stand before me in the gap on behalf of the land so I would not have to destroy it . . ." (Ezek. 22:30).

### FOR DISCUSSION

1. What has been central to God's program throughout history?

2. What part have institutions played in God's program?

3. What do you think it means when Christ says He is building the church?

4. How do you think He is building the church?

5. What part do you have in the building of the church?

6. Why do you think there is confusion over the mission of the church?

7. What do you think the mission of the church is?

# EPILOGUE

# CHAPTER 12

# WHAT IS THE NEXT STEP?

*Daniel and Lot both had lived in sinful cities: Daniel lived in Babylon, Lot lived in the twin cities of Sodom and Gomorrah. But there was a great difference—Lot not only lived in Sodom, but Sodom lived in him!*

Both Lot and Daniel were believers. Both were laymen. Both were living in cities synonymous with sin and degradation. But there the similarity ends. Daniel lived for God. Lot did not.

## Where Did Lot Go Wrong?

In Genesis 13 we read that Abraham and Lot divided the land. Abraham gave Lot the first choice and Lot took what looked like the choicest parcel. Genesis 13:12 says, "Abram lived in the land of Canaan, while Lot lived among the cities of the plain and pitched his tents *near Sodom.*"

The next time Lot is mentioned he is living *in Sodom* and is one of the leaders of the city (an excellent opportunity for a layman to glorify God). But the story of the decline and fall of Lot continues throughout Genesis 19. First, he loses the respect of the town. The people hold him in contempt. Next, he has no influence over his own family; they didn't believe or respect him. He is forced to flee Sodom, leaving behind all his riches. He takes only his wife and two unmarried daughters.

Genesis 19:26 is the familiar passage that tells us Lot lost his wife, when she looked back and was turned to a pillar of salt.

The last reference to Lot tells us he is living incestuously, in a drunken stupor, with his two daughters in a cave.

Yet second Peter 2:7 calls Lot a "righteous" man. The unfortunate thing is that this righteous believer was sucked up into the world's system and was destroyed, having little or no impact for God where he lived and worked.

## How Was Daniel Different?

Daniel, too, lived in a wretchedly sinful city—Babylon. He was a layman who had the opportunity to glorify God in an alien environment . . . and he did! He can be a model, for he did the very thing that faces all laymen in the midst of the marketplace who want to make an impact for Christ. How did Daniel survive and ably serve the Lord?

1. *He obeyed God.* Being a Jew, he was obligated to obey the laws of Moses, which said he shouldn't eat certain foods. Daniel 1:8: "But Daniel resolved not to defile himself with the royal food and wine, and he asked the chief official for permission not to defile himself this way." Acts 5:29 says, "Peter and the other apostles replied: 'We must obey God rather than men!'"

2. *He sought out fellowship with like-minded men* (Dan. 1:19). This was a small support group to help him in his quest to serve God. Jesus said in Matthew 18:20, "For where two or three come together in my name, there am I with them."

3. *He was a man of prayer.* He prayed three times daily as was *customary* for him. Prayer was forbidden, and it was for this act that he was thrown into the lions' den (Dan. 6:10). "The prayer of a righteous man is powerful and effective" (James 5:16).

4. *He was a man of the Word* (Dan. 9:2).

5. *He witnessed for God right where he was.* This was evident from the story of King Nebuchadnezzar, for whom Daniel worked.

Nebuchadnezzar was a proud and vain man. He gloried in the city he had built. He said, "Is not this the great Babylon I have built as the royal residence, by my mighty power and for the glory of my majesty?" (Dan. 4:30). When he made this self-glorifying statement he was struck with insanity that continued for seven years.

While Nebuchadnezzar was absent from the city, Babylon continued on as before, with no major changes. In other words, Nebuchadnezzar's personal "might" and "glory" weren't needed to keep the kingdom intact. But when the king was absent, especially for such a long period of time as seven years, ambitious men would take over the throne.

But he left Daniel in charge—godly Daniel. And Daniel kept the throne for Nebuchadnezzar. The God of Daniel was glorified. When Nebuchadnezzar returned from his insanity, he said, "I praised the Most High; I honored and glorified him who lives forever. His dominion is an eternal dominion; his kingdom endures from generation to generation. All the peoples of the earth are regarded as nothing. He does as he pleases with the powers of heaven and the peoples of the earth. No one can hold back his hand or say to him: 'What have you done?'" (Dan. 4:34–35).

Daniel lived in a sinful city, but he glorified God and served him right where he was. Lot's problem was not that he lived in Sodom, but that Sodom lived in him . . . and, undoubtedly, Sodom lived in Lot far longer than Lot lived in Sodom.

Evangelical Christianity is filled with Lots. They know the language, they go to the meetings . . . but they don't truly live for the things of God; they live for the things of the world. They are paper-thin Christians and the world sees right through them.

The excuse is not the times we live in; it is what lives within us.

May this book encourage you to be a Daniel who will live for God in the midst of the marketplace. And a key thing about Daniel was that he was alone. He did not have the support of institutions to assist him. The temple had been destroyed, the sacrificial system had been abolished, the priesthood was gone. Daniel did without the traditional support pattern the believer is accustomed to . . . and so can you as a lay person! You can do it in your community and city. You don't have to wait for a "super-preacher" or "super-church!"

Here are some suggestions about what can be done regarding the issues raised in this book. These are offered to individual lay men and women, to the leaders of the various assemblies, and to the "specialty group" leaders. These are all attitudinal responses that will help all three groups work more effectively together:

## Suggestions for Individual Lay Men and Women:

1. *You are a priest of God.* Realize that you, today, can begin working for Him in your sphere of influence. Don't think you can only serve Him when He furnishes you with a "super-church" or "super-preacher."
2. *Check chapter 4 to see if the marks of a spiritually maturing disciple are present in your life.* Do this on a regular basis.
3. *Have you put God in a box?* He is infinite. Have you put limits on Him? Ask Him to redi-

137

rect your thoughts so you can see Him in a more proper perspective.

4. *Learn about other ministries.* See what is happening beyond your own area of ministry interest. This will broaden your concept of God . . . and of the body of Christ . . . for you will see His glory revealed in a variety of ways.

5. *Expose yourself to the whole counsel of God.* Plan a personal Bible-study program with this concept in mind.

6. *Evaluate your expectations of your local fellowship.* Are these expectations consistent with its goals and capabilities? Adjust your expectations to reality. Trust God to meet your spiritual needs through other agencies if necessary.

7. *Discover the ministry vehicle best suited for your gifts.* Begin co-laboring to the unreached and uncommitted.

### Suggestions for Local Congregations and Pastors:

1. *Accept your organization's limitations.* No one person or one group can do it all. Realize this and accept that function that God has given you to do.

2. *Let "specialty groups" help you.* However, realize that your approach to the body of Christ will be on a somewhat broader base than they operate on.

3. *Don't compete.* Consciously and continuously withdraw from competition, whether it is ex-

pressed in numbers, budgets, buildings, or whatever. Instead, give of your facilities and programs to disciple men and women.

4. *Respect the individuality of each person.* Each individual will have different requirements to meet his or her specific needs at different points in time. Do not create a "super churchman" model to which you encourage all of your parishioners to conform.

5. *Don't force and regiment "body life."* It will occur spontaneously.

6. *Develop a community vision.* Rejoice that some, if not most, of this will occur outside the local assembly. This means becoming a servant to the process of spiritual growth of individuals. This may involve a willingness to give people away to other situations for a better opportunity for their true spiritual growth.

7. *Ask individuals how you can better minister to them.* Consciously avoid thinking of them in terms of what they can do for your institutional goals.

8. *Use of church renewal and church growth programs.* Use them carefully if the stated goal is the growth of your fellowship statistically. True concern for individuals could be subverted and the institution only could be benefited. Must be cautious here.

9. *Try some "high-risk'" ministries.* At least, experiment with some. These are ministries that subject you to potential criticism or have a high capability of risk of failure or which

promise very little numerical return to the institution in terms of membership or funds.

10. *Unselfishly minister to other groups.* Count it a privilege to minister to other Christian leaders without even thinking of how you can "involve" them in your local congregation. Let their involvement occur along natural lines, rather than in terms of "you ought to."

## Suggestions for Specialty Groups:

1. *Know yourself.* Realize that your particular mission is highly concentrated as far as focus is concerned and always seems more glamorous than the "nitty-gritty" of the local congregation.

2. *Handle newly acquired disciples responsibly.* Acknowledge that your mission will always "skim" talent and resources that denominations and assemblies would naturally desire to have available to them. This means you have a stewardship for these people to make sure they fit into the community, the body of Christ at large, in a healthy way that is edifying to the entire body.

3. *Realize your limitations with people.* Be aware that most specialty group missions have only concentrated short-term involvement in the lives of people and should be willing to let them flow back into other manifestations of the body of Christ when they feel the need to do so.

4. *Don't use people.* Acknowledge that you, as well as all organizations, have the continual

temptation to "use" people for their talent and resources. Be as cautious of doing this as you expect the pastor to be.

5. *Refrain from competing.* Refuse to put yourself in a threatening position with any pastor and withdraw from any spirit that seems competitive. Remember that the pastor will respond affirmatively when he sees produced through your means a better model than he is able to produce ... but this should not be a threat to him. Threatening postures are unscriptural and foreign to any New Testament concept of the body in operation.

6. *Depend upon God, not men.* You must never make the validity of your mission dependent, in your own mind or the mind of others, on the approval of a local pastor or group of pastors. Do what you do with the assurance of God's call, without waiting for the approval of men who have not ministered to you.

7. *You have great responsibility.* Remember that as a specialty group leader your Christian profile can become very high in the community, carrying with it great responsibility to model an effective, balanced and maturing Christian lifestyle within the community.

**FOR DISCUSSION**

1. Are you a Lot or Daniel? List the reasons why.

2. How can you change, if you are a Lot?

3. Of the several suggestions listed for your specific group, which are you already doing? How?

4. Which are you not doing? How can you take measurable steps to overcome these attitudinal habits?

5. Are there any suggestions we have omitted that you think would also be helpful?

6. How has this book most helped you in your Christian life?